# EFFECTIVE MEETING Skills

**LANGUAGE FOR SUCCESS**
Enhance business performance by acquiring practical business meeting and language skills.

CARROT HOUSE

**CARROT HOUSE**
P.O.Box #2924, St. Marys, Ontario, Canada

**Effective Meeting Skills**
© Carrot House

All rights reserved. No part of this publication may be reproduced, stored in a retrieval system, or transmitted in any form or by any means without the prior permission in writing of Carrot House

**Printed :** July 2019

**Author :** Carrot Language Lab

**ISBN** 978-89-6732-169-7

**Printed and distributed in Korea**
9F, 488, Gangnam St., Gangnam-gu, Seoul 06120, Korea

# Curriculum Map

| Course | Level 1 | Level 2 | Level 3 | Level 4 | Level 5 | Level 6 | Level 7 |
|---|---|---|---|---|---|---|---|
| **General Conversation** | Essential English: Begin Again | | | | | | |
| | Pre Get Up to Speed 1~2 | New Get Up to Speed 1 | | | | | |
| | | | New Get Up to Speed 2 | | | | |
| | | | | New Get Up to Speed 3 | | | |
| | | | | | New Get Up to Speed 4 | | |
| | | Daily Focused English 1 | | | | | |
| | | Daily Focused English 2 | | | | | |
| **Discussion** | | | | Active Discussion 1 | | | |
| | | | | | Active Discussion 2 | | |
| | | | | | | Dynamic Discussion | |
| | | | | Chicken Soup Course | | | |
| | | | | | Dynamic Information & Digital Technology | | |
| **Business Conversation** | Pre Business Basics 1 | | | | | | |
| | | Pre Business Basics 2 | | | | | |
| | | | Business Basics 1 | | | | |
| | | | | Business Basics 2 | | | |
| | | | | | Business Practice 1 | | |
| | | | | | | Business Practice 2 | |
| **Global Biz Workshop** | | | | Effective Business Writing Skills (Workbook) | | | |
| | | | | Effective Presentation Skills (Workbook) | | | |
| | | | | | Effective Negotiation Skills (Workbook) | | |
| | | | | | Cross-Cultural Training 1~2 (Workbook) | | |
| | | | | | Leadership Training Course (Workbook) | | |
| **Business Skills** | | | | Simple & Clear Technical Writing Skills | | | |
| | | | | Effective Business Writing Skills | | | |
| | | | | Effective Meeting Skills | | | |
| | | | | Business Communication (Negotiation) | | | |
| | | | | Effective Presentation Skills | | | |
| | | | | | Marketing 1 | | |
| | | | | | | Marketing 2 | |
| | | | | | | Management | |
| **On the Job English** | | | | Human Resources | | | |
| | | | | Accounting and Finance | | | |
| | | | | Marketing and Sales | | | |
| | | | | Production Management | | | |
| | | | | Automotive | | | |
| | | | | Banking and Commerce | | | |
| | | | | Medical and Medicine | | | |
| | | | | Information Technology | | | |
| | | | | Construction | | | |
| | | | Construction English in Use 1~4 | | | | |
| | | | Public Service English in Use | | | | |

※ This Curriculum Map illustrates the entire line-up of textbooks at CARROT HOUSE.

# Effective Meeting Skills

## Introduction

### Carrot House Methodology
Andragogical Approach & Productive English

The teaching of children (pedagogy) and adult learning (andragogy) are distinctively different. Pedagogy is akin to training and encourages convergent thinking and rote learning. It is compulsory, centered on the teacher and the imparting of information with minimal control by the learner. Andragogy, by contrast, is about education as freedom. It encourages divergent thinking and active learning. It is voluntary, learner oriented and opens up vistas for continuing learning. Adults need to feel independent and in control of their learning. Therefore, Carrot House curriculum is based on andragogy and is designed to encourage learners' participation and engagement by providing more task-based activities and opportunities to frequently interact in the classroom.

People want to achieve communicative competence when they learn other languages. English education in EFL environments has been rather focused on the receptive skills of English—listening and reading—which simply increases learners' knowledge about a language, not the competence of using it. If people are well equipped with productive skills—speaking and writing—they will be competent in English communication.

This is why Carrot House curriculum is designed to enhance learners' productive skills throughout the course. This andragogical approach of the Carrot House Curriculum, which focuses on productive English, will enable learners to achieve communication skills necessary for global competence. Carrot House's teaching philosophy and curriculum combine to provide a "Language for Success" for all learners.

### Communicative Language Learning (CLL)

This communicative interaction, the essential component of language acquisition, does not occur in a typical, non-meaningful, fun-oriented conversation with native speakers. It occurs in a negotiated interaction through which a well-trained teacher provides the comprehensible input that is appropriate to the learners. The learners, at the same time, actively utilize the opportunities given to them by the teachers.

To this end, the Communicative Language Learning (CLL) method is employed in the field of Foreign Language Acquisition. The CLL method provides activities that are geared toward using language pragmatically, authentically and functionally with the intention of achieving meaningful purposes.

# User's Guide

## Overview
Effective Meeting Skills is intended to improve learners' business performance through acquiring practical business meeting and language skills. From examining the basic structure of business meetings through to practical meeting skills, the key aspects of business meetings are studied to help learners polish and master their understanding of business meetings. Through case studies of various different business meeting types, learners will enhance meetings skills that are relevant to the practical demands of the business world.

## Chapter Composition

### Chapter 1 - 6
The textbook is divided into three different chapter structures. Chapters 1 - 6 focus on the planning, proceeding, and follow-up of business meetings. Chapters 7 - 11 introduce various meeting skills required in the international business field. Finally, the simulations placed between each chapter gives practical case studies on different types of business meetings.

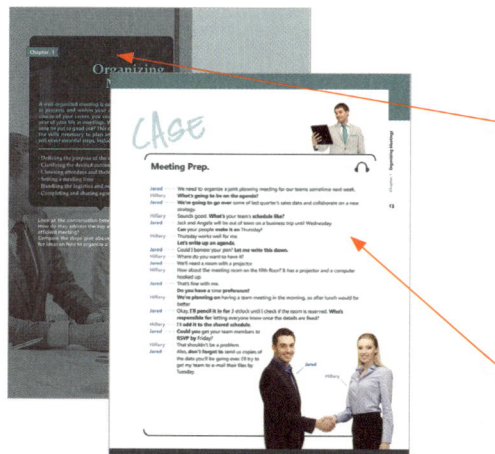

**1. Introduction**
Each chapter opens up with an introduction to the meeting structure or skill to be learned. This provides not only a general understanding of the topic but also gives the chapter's learning objectives.

**2. Case**
The case is a transcript of a conversation that takes place within a meeting. This provides an example of an ideal meeting conversation and the use of meeting skills.

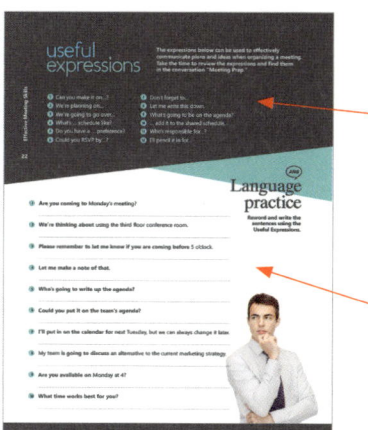

**3. Useful Expressions**
Each chapter consists of a list of useful expressions. The expressions are used in the 'Case' providing examples of how to effectively use the language.

**4. Language Practice**
The 'Useful Expressions' of each chapter can be practiced in this section.

# Effective Meeting Skills

### 5. How to...

The 'How to...' section of each chapter introduces the meeting skills relevant to the chapter's topic. The activity reviews the skills need for the meeting proceedings and provides an area to discuss and analyze the problems that occur in daily meetings.

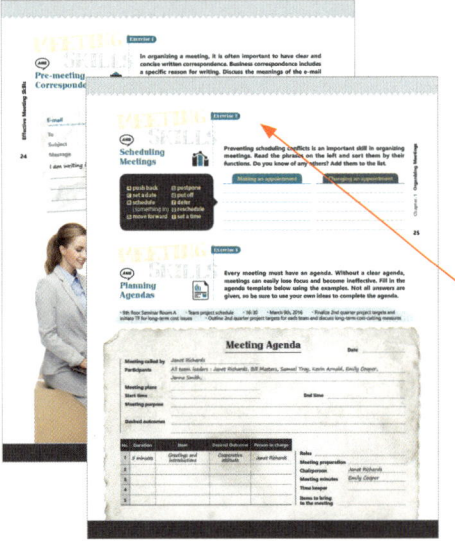

### 6. Meeting Skills 1, 2, 3

Each chapter consists of three meeting skills. Each activity allows for learners to practice utilizing the skills required for effective meetings.

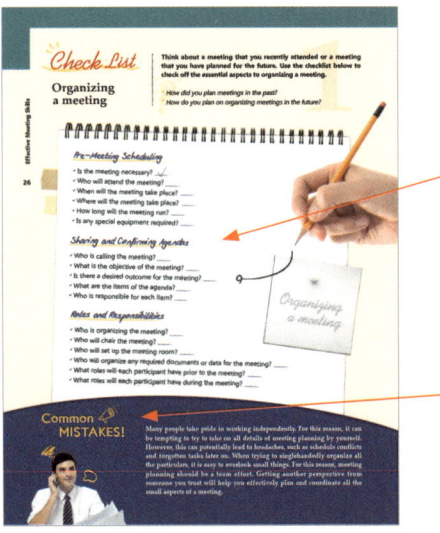

### 7. Checklist

The checklist at the end of each chapter allows for learners to review the steps and skills required in meetings. Each checklist is designed specifically to follow the requirements of the chapters' meeting procedures.

### 8. Common Mistakes

This section allows for participants to recognize and review common mistakes made by business people.

# Chapter 7 - 11

### 1. Have You Ever...
Each chapter opens with a hypothetical worst case scenario that arises when a meeting skill is ignored or inappropriately used. This introduction is for learners to be able to relate to the skills that are addressed in the chapter.

### 2. What Should You Do?
Based on the 'Have you ever...' scenario, learners are provided with open ended discussion questions to find solutions to the problems that arise during ineffective meetings.

### 3. A Gentleman Says...
This section allows to learners to compare and contrast the differences between effective and ineffective meeting language.

### 4. Meeting Skills 1, 2
Each chapter is comprised of two meeting skills. Each skill is studied through the following two sections.

**What is it?**
This gives an overview of the skill.

**How To...**
This provides an area to practice the application of the meeting skill.

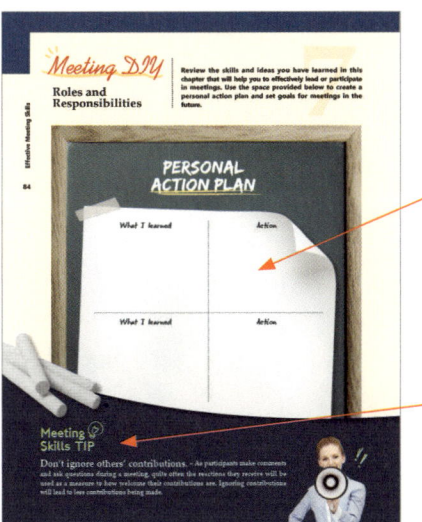

### 5. Meeting DIY
Each chapter closes with an area to review the key aspects of the lesson. In addition, an area to create a personal action plan is given to help learners apply the skills learned through the chapter.

### 6. Meeting Skills TIP
This section gives learners good to know tips for conducting effective meetings.

# Effective Meeting Skills

## Simulations 1 - 10

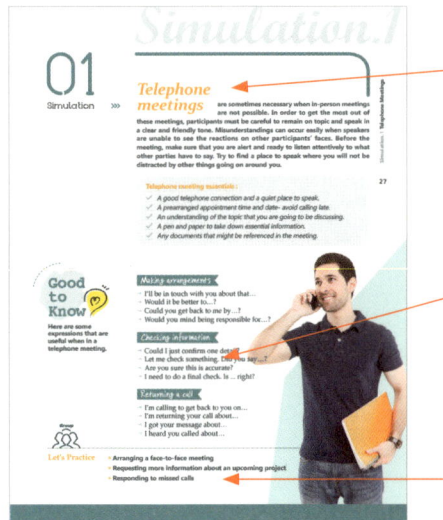

### 1. Introduction
Each simulation opens up with an introduction to the meeting style to be studied. This section provides an overview of what specific features make the meeting different from other forms of meetings.

### 2. Good To Know
This section provides a list of key expressions that can be used in the chapter's meeting style.

### 3. Let's Practice
This section provides situations in which the key expressions can be used and practiced by learners.

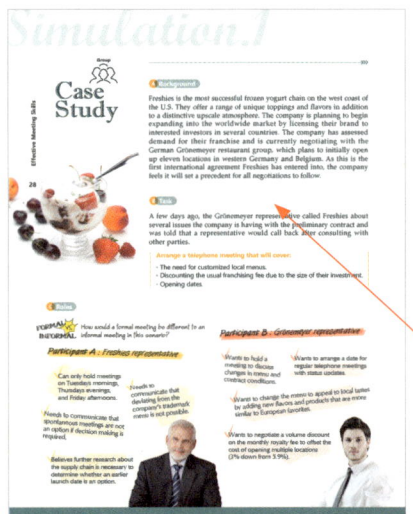

### 4. CASE STUDY
This section provides a case study for learners to role play and apply meeting skills and languages. Learners are given the necessary information and roles to complete the given tasks. The section is divided into three parts.

- **Background**
  This provides information required for learners to understand the setting and the history of the meeting that is to take place.
- **Task**
  This provides the meeting's objectives and an overview of the agenda.
- **Roles**
  This gives the different perspectives of the meeting's participants and also what each participant wants to achieve through the meeting.

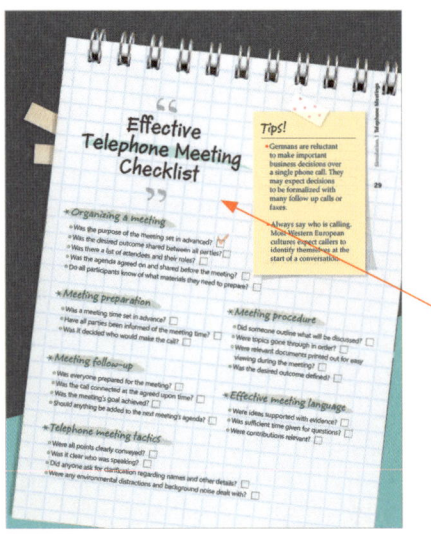

### 5. Effective Meeting Checklist
This section is provided for learners to use as a self or peer checklist activity. The checklist is to evaluate learners understanding of the elements of an effective meeting.

# Contents

| Chapter | Learning Objectives | Meeting Skills | Page |
|---|---|---|---|
| 1. Organizing Meetings | - Defining the purpose of the meeting<br>- Clarifying the desired outcomes<br>- Choosing attendees and their roles<br>- Setting a meeting time<br>- Handling the logistics and necessary preparation<br>- Completing and sharing agendas | 1. Pre-meeting Correspondence<br>2. Scheduling Meetings<br>3. Planning Agendas | 12 |
| | **Telephone Meetings**<br>CASE : Freshies & Grönemeyer | | 19 |
| 2. Opening Meetings | - Greetings and introductions<br>- Reviewing meeting purpose<br>- Clarifying roles and responsibilities (R&R)<br>- Checking agendas | 1. Greetings and introductions<br>2. Agenda<br>3. Roles | 22 |
| | **Conference Calls**<br>CASE : Fairmont Industries & Qatar Constructions | | 29 |
| 3. Meeting Procedures | - Presenting ideas<br>- Participating in discussions<br>- Giving and responding to opinions<br>- Following meeting procedures | 1. Presentations<br>2. Discussions<br>3. Following Procedures | 32 |
| | **Annual General Meetings**<br>CASE : Mulhouse and Reimes | | 39 |
| 4. Meeting Communication | - Asking for clarification<br>- Asking for comments and contributions<br>- Responding to offers and suggestions<br>- Dealing with interruptions | 1. Clarifying<br>2. Comments and Contributions<br>3. Handling Interruptions | 42 |
| | **Damage Control Meetings**<br>CASE : Masuka Industrials | | 49 |
| 5. Closing Meetings | - Summarizing the proceedings<br>- Reaching a consensus on issues from the meeting<br>- Evaluating the meeting<br>- Organizing action plans for meeting follow-up | 1. Summarizing the discussion<br>2. Reaching a consensus<br>3. Evaluating the meeting | 52 |
| | **Progress Report Meetings**<br>CASE : Evermore Productions | | 59 |
| 6. Meeting Follow-up | - Writing meeting minutes<br>- Sharing meeting minutes<br>- Checking action plans | 1. Writing Meeting Minutes<br>2. Meeting Minutes Do's & Don'ts<br>3. Sharing Meeting Minutes | 62 |
| | **Project Initiation Meetings**<br>CASE : Hotel La Cep & Bayeux Design | | 69 |

# Effective Meeting Skills

## Table of Contents

| Chapter | Learning Objectives | Meeting Skills | Page |
|---|---|---|---|
| 7 — Roles and Responsibilities | - Recognize different behaviors expected for different meeting roles<br>- Understand the responsibilities that follow various roles | 1. Facilitating a meeting<br>2. Host vs. Guest | 73 |
| | **Brainstorming Meetings**<br>CASE : Buzz Cola & Bharat Group | | 77 |
| 8 — Setting and Environment | - Recognize suitable meeting location settings based on the meeting's purpose<br>- Recognize the influence held by the atmosphere and environment of a meeting | 1. Meeting Room Layout<br>2. Break Time Conversation | 81 |
| | **Decision-making Meetings**<br>CASE : AXA | | 85 |
| 9 — Writing Technique | - Understand the importance of accurate and clear written materials<br>- Learn skills required to prepare written materials | 1. Presentation and Handout materials<br>2. Meeting Minutes | 89 |
| | **Consultations**<br>CASE : Navisoft & Harrison PR Solutions | | 93 |
| 10 — Meeting Etiquette | - Recognize good business etiquette<br>- Learn key skills for maintaining meeting etiquette | 1. Making apologies<br>2. Interruptions | 97 |
| | **Negotiations**<br>CASE : Haoyuan China Limited & Municipal | | 101 |
| 11 — Cross-Cultural Skills | - Recognize the impact of cultural differences on holding effective international meetings | 1. Punctuality across cultures<br>2. Dealing with differences | 105 |

| Appendix | |
|---|---|
| **Key Expressions** | 110 |
| **Answer Key** | 119 |

**01** Organizing Meetings **12**
**02** Opening Meetings **22**
**03** Meeting Procedures **32**
**04** Meeting Communication **42**
**05** Closing Meetings **52**
**06** Meeting Follow-up **62**
**07** Roles and Responsibilities **73**
**08** Setting and Environment **81**
**09** Writing Technique **89**
**10** Meeting Etiquette **97**
**11** Cross-Cultural Skills **105**
**Appendix 110**

# Effective Meeting Skills

**Chapter. 1**

# Organizing Meetings

A well-organized meeting is essential for success both in projects and within your organization. Over the course of your career, you could spend as much as a year of your life in meetings. Wouldn't you prefer this time be put to good use? This chapter aims to give you the skills necessary to plan an efficient meeting and will cover essential steps, including :

› Defining the purpose of the meeting
› Clarifying the desired outcomes
› Choosing attendees and their roles
› Setting a meeting time
› Handling the logistics and necessary preparation
› Completing and sharing agendas

Look at the conversation between Jared and Hillary. How do they address the key elements to planning an efficient meeting?
Compare the steps give above with the conversation for ideas on how to organize a meeting.

》》》

## Meeting Prep.

**Jared** — We need to organize a joint planning meeting for our teams sometime next week.
**Hillary** — **What's going to be on the agenda?**
**Jared** — **We're going to go over** some of last quarter's sales data and collaborate on a new strategy.
**Hillary** — Sounds good. **What's** your team's **schedule like?**
**Jared** — Jack and Angela will be out of town on a business trip until Wednesday. **Can** your people **make it on** Thursday?
**Hillary** — Thursday works well for me. **Let's write up an agenda.**
**Jared** — Could I borrow your pen? **Let me write this down.**
**Hillary** — Where do you want to have it?
**Jared** — We'll need a room with a projector.
**Hillary** — How about the meeting room on the fifth floor? It has a projector and a computer hooked up.
**Jared** — That's fine with me. **Do you have a** time **preference?**
**Hillary** — **We're planning on** having a team meeting in the morning, so after lunch would be better.
**Jared** — Okay. **I'll pencil it in for** 3 o'clock until I check if the room is reserved. **Who's responsible for** letting everyone know once the details are fixed?
**Hillary** — I'll **add it to the shared schedule**.
**Jared** — **Could you** get your team members to **RSVP by** Friday?
**Hillary** — That shouldn't be a problem.
**Jared** — Also, **don't forget to** send us copies of the data you'll be going over. I'll try to get my team to e-mail their files by Tuesday.

Jared
Hillary

## useful expressions

The expressions below can be used to effectively communicate plans and ideas when organizing a meeting. Take the time to review the expressions and find them in the CASE "Meeting Prep."

1. Can you make it on...?
2. We're planning on...
3. We're going to go over...
4. What's ... schedule like?
5. Do you have a ... preference?
6. Could you RSVP by...?
7. Don't forget to...
8. Let me write this down.
9. What's going to be on the agenda?
10. ... add it to the shared schedule.
11. Who's responsible for...?
12. I'll pencil it in for...

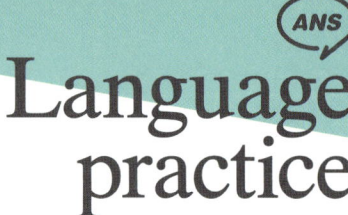

## Language practice

Reword and write the sentences using the Useful Expressions.

1. **Are you coming to** Monday's meeting?

2. **We're thinking about** using the third floor conference room.

3. **Please remember to let me know if you are coming before** 5 o'clock.

4. Let me make a note of that.

5. Who's going to write up the agenda?

6. Could you put it on the team's agenda?

7. **I'll put in on the calendar for** next Tuesday, but we can always change it later.

8. My team **is going to discuss** an alternative to the current marketing strategy.

9. **Are you available on** Monday at 4?

10. What time works best for you?

# How to

## Theoretically

## Organize a meeting

Good meetings aren't accidents; they are the result of good planning. When deciding to hold a meeting, the first question you should ask is: 'Do we need to have a meeting?' Meetings are very useful in getting immediate reactions, resolving conflicts, tapping into the ideas of others, and ensuring the understanding of concepts and tasks. However, meetings should not be called for when there is no concrete need. Assuming that a meeting is necessary, let's have a look at the major elements that are essential in planning a meeting.

**Group Application**

What are the points you need to consider when arranging the six elements for organizing a meeting?
Discuss and share your ideas in groups.

### Purpose
Every meeting must have a purpose. The meeting's purpose statement explains why the meeting is being held.

### Desired outcome
A desired outcome can be something that is tangible, such as a written plan, or intangible, including new knowledge or information.

### Attendees and roles
A list of the people required to attend the meeting to accomplish the objective must be predetermined along with each attendees' roles and responsibilities.

### Meeting times
A suitable time for the meeting considering all factors such as the availability of attendees, the time required for preparation, and the location.

### Logistics and preparation
The location must have the necessary equipment and layout to execute the meeting. Also, any preparation needed for the meeting must be shared to the right people.

### Agendas
As early as possible, a written agenda should be sent to all attendees. It's good to check with the attendees to confirm attendance and their expectations for the meeting.

- Purpose
- Desired outcome
- Attendees and roles
- Meeting times
- Logistics and preparation
- Agendas

# MEETING SKILLS

## Pre-meeting Correspondence

### Exercise 1

In organizing a meeting, it is often important to have clear and concise written correspondence. Business correspondence includes a specific reason for writing. Discuss the meanings of the e-mail openings and complete each sentence. In what situation could each e-mail opening be used?

**E-mail**
To:
Subject:
Message:
I am writing in response to …

**E-mail**
To:
Subject:
Message:
I am writing to confirm …

**E-mail**
To:
Subject:
Message:
I am writing to apologize for …

**E-mail**
To:
Subject:
Message:
I am writing to inform you …

**E-mail**
To:
Subject:
Message:
I am writing regarding …

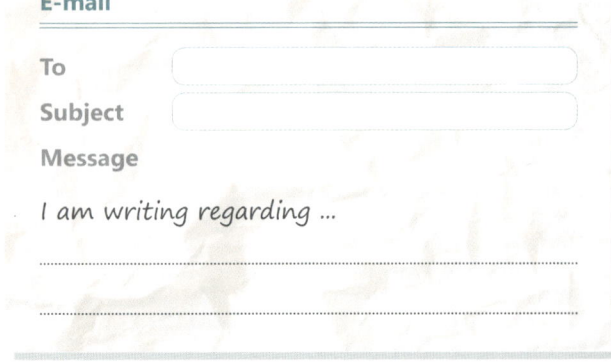

# MEETING SKILLS

### Exercise 2

## Scheduling Meetings

Preventing scheduling conflicts is an important skill in organizing meetings. Read the phrases on the left and sort them by their functions. Do you know of any others? Add them to the list.

- a push back
- b postpone
- c set a date
- d put off
- e schedule (something in)
- f defer
- g reschedule
- h move forward
- i set a time

| Making an appointment | Changing an appointment |
|---|---|
| | |
| | |
| | |

---

# MEETING SKILLS

### Exercise 3

## Planning Agendas

Every meeting must have an agenda. Without a clear agenda, meetings can easily lose focus and become ineffective. Fill in the agenda template below using the examples. Not all answers are given, so be sure to use your own ideas to complete the agenda.

- ◆ 9th floor Seminar Room A
- ◆ Team project schedule
- ◆ 16:30
- ◆ March 9th, 2016
- ◆ Finalize 2nd quarter project targets and initiate TF for long-term cost issues
- ◆ Outline 2nd quarter project targets for each team and discuss long-term cost-cutting measures

## Meeting Agenda

**Date** _____

**Meeting called by**: Janet Richards

**Participants**: All team leaders : Janet Richards, Bill Masters, Samuel Troy, Kevin Arnold, Emily Cooper, Jenna Smith,

**Meeting place**: _____

**Start time**: _____   **End time**: _____

**Meeting purpose**: _____

**Desired outcomes**: _____

| No. | Duration | Item | Desired Outcome | Person in charge |
|---|---|---|---|---|
| 1 | 5 minutes | Greetings and introductions | Cooperative attitude | Janet Richards |
| 2 | | | | |
| 3 | | | | |
| 4 | | | | |
| 5 | | | | |

**Roles**

- Meeting preparation: _____
- Chairperson: Janet Richards
- Meeting minutes: Emily Cooper
- Time keeper: _____
- Items to bring to the meeting: _____

# Check List

## Organizing a meeting

**Think about a meeting that you recently attended or a meeting that you have planned for the future. Use the checklist below to check off the essential aspects to organizing a meeting.**

» *How did you plan meetings in the past?*
» *How do you plan on organizing meetings in the future?*

### Pre-Meeting Scheduling

- Is the meeting necessary? ✓
- Who will attend the meeting? ____
- When will the meeting take place? ____
- Where will the meeting take place? ____
- How long will the meeting run? ____
- Is any special equipment required? ____

### Sharing and Confirming Agendas

- Who is calling the meeting? ____
- What is the objective of the meeting? ____
- Is there a desired outcome for the meeting? ____
- What are the items of the agenda? ____
- Who is responsible for each item? ____

### Roles and Responsibilities

- Who is organizing the meeting? ____
- Who will chair the meeting? ____
- Who will set up the meeting room? ____
- Who will organize any required documents or data for the meeting? ____
- What roles will each participant have prior to the meeting? ____
- What roles will each participant have during the meeting? ____

## Common MISTAKES!

Many people take pride in working independently. For this reason, it can be tempting to try to take on all details of meeting planning by yourself. However, this can potentially lead to headaches, such as schedule conflicts and forgotten tasks later on. When trying to singlehandedly organize all the particulars, it is easy to overlook small things. For this reason, meeting planning should be a team effort. Getting another perspective from someone you trust will help you effectively plan and coordinate all the small aspects of a meeting.

# 01 Simulation ›› Telephone meetings

**Telephone meetings** are sometimes necessary when in-person meetings are not possible. In order to get the most out of these meetings, participants must be careful to remain on topic and speak in a clear and friendly tone. Misunderstandings can occur easily when speakers are unable to see the reactions on other participants' faces. Before the meeting, make sure that you are alert and ready to listen attentively to what other parties have to say. Try to find a place to speak where you will not be distracted by other things going on around you.

**Telephone meeting essentials :**
- ✓ A good telephone connection and a quiet place to speak.
- ✓ A prearranged appointment time and date; avoid calling late.
- ✓ An understanding of the topic that you are going to be discussing.
- ✓ A pen and paper to take down essential information.
- ✓ Any documents that might be referenced in the meeting.

## Good to Know

Here are some expressions that are useful when in a telephone meeting.

### Making arrangements
- I'll be in touch with you about that…
- Would it be better to…?
- Could you get back to me by…?
- Would you mind being responsible for…?

### Checking information
- Could I just confirm one detail?
- Let me check something. Did you say…?
- Are you sure this is accurate?
- I need to do a final check. Is … right?

### Returning a call
- I'm calling to get back to you on…
- I'm returning your call about…
- I got your message about…
- I heard you called about…

## Let's Practice (Group)
» Arranging a face-to-face meeting
» Requesting more information about an upcoming project
» Responding to missed calls

# Simulation.1

*Effective Meeting Skills*

## Case Study

### A. Background

Freshies is the most successful frozen yogurt chain on the west coast of the U.S. They offer a range of unique toppings and flavors in addition to a distinctive upscale atmosphere. The company is planning to begin expanding into the worldwide market by licensing their brand to interested investors in several countries. The company has assessed demand for their franchise and is currently negotiating with the German Grönemeyer restaurant group, which plans to initially open up eleven locations in western Germany and Belgium. As this is the first international agreement Freshies has entered into, the company feels it will set a precedent for all negotiations to follow.

### B. Task

A few days ago, the Grönemeyer representative called Freshies about several issues the company is having with the preliminary contract and was told that a representative would call back after consulting with other parties.

> **Arrange a telephone meeting that will cover:**
> - The need for customized local menus.
> - Discounting the usual franchising fee due to the size of their investment.
> - Opening dates.

### C. Roles

**FORMAL vs. INFORMAL** — How would a formal meeting be different to an informal meeting in this scenario?

**Participant A : Freshies representative**

- ✓ Can only hold meetings on Tuesdays mornings, Thursdays evenings, and Friday afternoons.
- ✓ Needs to communicate that deviating from the company's trademark menu is not possible.
- ✓ Needs to communicate that spontaneous meetings are not an option if decision making is required.
- ✓ Believes further research about the supply chain is necessary to determine whether an earlier launch date is an option.

**Participant B : Grönemeyer representative**

- ✓ Wants to hold a meeting to discuss changes in menu and contract conditions.
- ✓ Wants to arrange a date for regular telephone meetings with status updates.
- ✓ Wants to change the menu to appeal to local tastes by adding new flavors and products that are more similar to European favorites.
- ✓ Wants to negotiate a volume discount on the monthly royalty fee to offset the cost of opening multiple locations (3% down from 5.9%).

# " Effective Telephone Meeting Checklist "

### *Organizing a meeting
- Was the purpose of the meeting set in advanced? ✓
- Was the desired outcome shared between all parties? ☐
- Was there a list of attendees and their roles? ☐
- Was the agenda agreed on and shared before the meeting? ☐
- Do all participants know of what materials they need to prepare? ☐

### *Meeting preparation
- Was a meeting time set in advance? ☐
- Have all parties been informed of the meeting time? ☐
- Was it decided who would make the call? ☐

### *Meeting follow-up
- Was everyone prepared for the meeting? ☐
- Was the call connected at the agreed upon time? ☐
- Was the meeting's goal achieved? ☐
- Should anything be added to the next meeting's agenda? ☐

### *Telephone meeting tactics
- Were all points clearly conveyed? ☐
- Was it clear who was speaking? ☐
- Did anyone ask for clarification regarding names and other details? ☐
- Were any environmental distractions and background noise dealt with? ☐

### *Meeting procedure
- Did someone outline what will be discussed? ☐
- Were topics gone through in order? ☐
- Were relevant documents printed out for easy viewing during the meeting? ☐
- Was the desired outcome defined? ☐

### *Effective meeting language
- Were ideas supported with evidence? ☐
- Was sufficient time given for questions? ☐
- Were contributions relevant? ☐

---

**Tips!**

- Germans are reluctant to make important business decisions over a single phone call. They may expect decisions to be formalized with many follow up calls or faxes.

- Always say who is calling. Most Western European cultures expect callers to identify themselves at the start of a conversation.

**Chapter. 2**

# Opening Meetings

The start of a meeting is just as important as the planning that went into it. went into it. The opening sets the pace and tone for the meeting—something that ultimately impacts the end result of the proceedings. This chapter aims to provide you with the background to effectively manage the opening of a meeting. We will cover crucial aspects of the process, including :

› Greetings and introductions
› Reviewing meeting purpose
› Clarifying roles and responsibilities(R&R)
› Checking agendas

Look at the conversation between Mr. Preston, John, and Mallory. How do they address the key elements to opening a meeting?
Compare the steps give above with the conversation for ideas on how to open a meeting.

»>

## Getting Started.

| | |
|---|---|
| John | Thank you all for coming. **I'd like to start by welcoming** a special visitor. We have Mr. Preston visiting from our branch in Shanghai. Welcome. |
| Mr. Preston | Thank you for the warm welcome. |
| John | Now, **if I can get your attention** again, **let's get down to business**. I've **called this meeting to** review our current marketing strategy and focus on making some schedule changes as requested by the Shanghai branch. But first, Mallory, could you give us a review of the last meeting's proceedings, and Jack, **could you take the minutes?** |
| Mallory | Right, **let me begin with** the previous meeting's minutes. Our last quarterly marketing meeting was held on July 7$^{th}$ with all ten members of the TF* present. The meeting was opened at 16:00 by John, who was chairing the meeting. The previous meeting's minutes were reviewed by the secretary and the agenda included two items. |
| Mr. Preston | Sorry for interrupting, **could you remind me what** the two items were? |
| Mallory | They were the production schedule and the distribution issues. Moving on, the meeting was concluded at 17:30 with all items on the agenda reviewed and the minutes shared by Jack. |
| John | Thank you. That sounds good. Now, if there are no additional remarks, **I'd like to briefly go over** the agenda for today's meeting. **Have you all seen a copy of the agenda?** Mr. Preston? |
| Mr. Preston | Yes, agenda number two. I don't think I was informed of this. **When was this** agenda **finalized?** |
| Mallory | On Thursday, I sent an e-mail. |
| Mr. Preston | I must have missed it. Please, continue. |
| John | I would like **to aim for a** three o'clock **finish**, so let's try to keep it brief. Could everyone please **direct your attention to** page 7 of the handout? |

***TF** : Task Force

# useful expressions

The expressions below can be used to effectively open a meeting. Take the time to review the expressions and find them in the CASE "Getting Started."

1. I'd like to start by welcoming…
2. If I can get your attention…
3. Let's get down to business.
4. … called this meeting to…
5. …, could you take the minutes?
6. Let me begin with…
7. Could you remind me what…?
8. I'd like to briefly go over…
9. Have you all seen a copy of the agenda?
10. When was this … finalized?
11. … to aim for a … finish.
12. … direct your attention to…

# Language practice

**Fill in the blanks to complete the sentences using the Useful Expressions.**

1. I'm sorry to interrupt, _____ time this meeting is expected to finish?

2. _____ our visitors from the Australian Branch. Mr. Jones, it's an honor to have you here.

3. Now that I have your attention, _____ the first item on the agenda.

4. As you are all aware, I've _____ deal with some recent problems that have occurred in the customer service department.

5. Could I _____ the 4th item on the agenda? I think it would be better to start with this first.

6. _____ I'd like to get the meeting started.

7. Before we continue I'd like to clarify our roles for this meeting, Paul, _____ _____?

8. _____? If there are no questions, let's get straight into it. We want _____ 3pm.

9. Now that everyone is here and settled, _____.

10. Before we look into the first item, _____ the modified budget for the second quarter.

# How to

## Theoretically

## Open a meeting

How should you start a meeting? A great start is crucial in giving a push to reach an excellent finish. In the opening minutes of a meeting, the tone and pace for the entire meeting are set. This tone and pace essentially become the cornerstone for the proceedings of the meeting. At the start of any meeting, there are a few items that should be dealt with to ensure high productivity throughout the entire meeting.

**Application** (Group)

What are the points you need to consider when you are preparing the four elements to opening a meeting?
Discuss and share your ideas in groups.

### Greetings
Greetings automatically provide an atmosphere where all members can interact and participate more freely in the meeting. Providing introductions will also help attendees recognize the key players of the meeting and connect the desired outcomes of the meeting to why each member is present.

### Purpose
The purpose of the meeting that was set during the preparation stage must be emphasized before the meeting proceedings begin. Stating the purpose is a crucial step as it helps guide the meeting to reach the desired outcome.

### Roles
The roles of attendees must also be clarified during the opening minutes of a meeting. It makes sure there is no confusion on what each attendee is expected to do during the meeting. Remember that all meeting attendees must be aware of who is doing what.

### Agendas
Reviewing the agenda at the start of a meeting helps keep things on track. Make sure that any changes or issues regarding the agenda are dealt with early on.

## Greetings and Introductions

### Exercise 1

Just as first impressions are very important, having a good start is crucial in setting the tone for the entire meeting. Doing business calls for flexibility. Choosing suitable business greetings and introductions for different business situations is a very valuable skill. In the space provided below, brainstorm suitable greetings for each category.

## Agenda

### Exercise 2

The following is a table consisting of estimate times to be allocated to different agenda items. Review the table and use it to create an agenda for a meeting of your choice.

### Time Estimations

- **Reviewing meeting purpose and agenda** - *5 to 10 minutes*
- **Information reports** - *5 to 10 minutes*
- **Questions regarding information reports** - *5 to 10 minutes*
- **Problem solving** : Define the problem - *15 to 30 minutes*
- **Problem solving** : List possible causes - *20 to 30 minutes*
- **Problem solving** : List solutions - *20 to 50 minutes*
- **Problem solving** : Create an action plan - *20 to 40 minutes*
- **Planning** : Define the task - *10 to 30 minutes*
- **Planning** : List activities and create an action plan - *30 to 90 minutes*
- **Planning** : Review the plan for obstacles - *30 to 60 minutes*
- **Decision-making** : Define the decision to be made - *10 to 15 minutes*
- **Decision-making** : Determine criteria and evaluate options - *15 to 60 minutes*
- **Decision-making** : Create action plan steps - *10 to 30 minutes*
- **Meeting summary and wrap up** - *5 to 10 minutes*

# Creating an agenda

| | ITEM | Duration | Desired Results | Person Responsible |
|---|---|---|---|---|
| 1 | | | | |
| 2 | | | | |
| 3 | | | | |
| 4 | | | | |
| 5 | | | | |
| 6 | | | | |

## Roles

### Exercise 3

Group roles or functions are tasks that can be shared by several people at the meeting. The tasks should be designated ahead of time and announced again at the start of a meeting. Providing clear R&R at the start of a meeting helps bring awareness to all attendees of their roles and duties during the meeting. The following are some roles that can be given to attendees of meetings. Match the roles with their duties and add to the list.

|  | |  |
|---|---|---|
| Chairperson | ○——○ | Keeps a written record of the meeting proceedings |
| Participant | ○——○ | Convenes the meeting and takes responsibility in communication before and after the meeting; leads discussions on the items of the meeting |
| Timekeeper | ○——○ | Contributes items to meeting agenda and shares ideas in team discussions, brainstorming and the proceedings of the meeting |
| Facilitator | ○——○ | Keeps the discussion and decision-making process moving by assisting the designated chairperson in accomplishing tasks and attending to group proceedings |
| Recorder | ○——○ | Keeps track of time and reminds the group of planned start and stop times for agenda items |
| .................. | ○——○ | .................. |
| .................. | ○——○ | .................. |

# Check List

## Opening meeting

**Think about a meeting that you recently attended or a meeting that you have planned for the future. Use the checklist below to check off the essential aspects to opening a meeting.**

» How did you open meetings in the past?
» How do you plan on opening meetings in the future?

### Greetings and Introductions
→ Were all attendees welcomed? ✓
→ Was there an icebreaker or warm up activity? ____
→ Were all visitors properly introduced? ____
→ Were any ground rules (if necessary) set for the meeting? ____

### Roles of Attendees
→ Were the roles clearly defined? ____
→ Were the attendees with designated roles aware of their duties? ____
→ Was someone tasked with recording the minutes? ____
→ Was there a designated leader? ____

### Outlining Agendas
→ Was the purpose of the meeting clarified? ____
→ Was the desired outcome defined? ____
→ Was the agenda shared to all attendees? ____
→ Were any changes or issues regarding the agenda sorted? ____
→ Was a finishing time for the meeting set in advance? ____

*Opening Meetings*

## Common MISTAKES!

One common mistake made by many meeting chairs is that they do not make the finalized agenda and the meeting's desired results clear from the start. This can result in confusion and a disorganized meeting. A way to overcome this is by taking a few minutes during the opening of the meeting to review roles, the agenda, and to remind everyone of the desired outcome of the meeting to keep everyone on the right track.

# 02 Simulation »»»

## Conference calls

are meetings that are conducted via telephone or online video network services. involve multiple parties communicating remotely from different locations. These meetings are common when collaborating with distant partners who are unable to physically attend meetings. Conference call meetings typically start with the organizing party dialing each participant individually and connecting their line to the call or with the attendants calling in directly using a conference bridge (equipment that connects telephone lines.) Doing business over a network service poses several unique challenges, such as extreme time differences and difficulty communicating points without clear visual context. As a result, successful conference recalls require both strong communication skills and meeting planning expertise.

**There are several problems that can negatively affect the success of conference calls :**

- ✓ People failing to answer.
- ✓ Unfamiliarity with procedures and expected behavior.
- ✓ Not appointing a moderator.
- ✓ Problems with equipment and technology.
- ✓ Background noise or a poor connection.
- ✓ Failure to coordinate in advance.

**Here are some expressions that are useful when holding conference calls.**

### Checking a word
- Is that … as in…?
- Could you spell that back to me?
- I'm sorry, but how do you spell that?
- Would you mind spelling that for me?

### Asking about plans
- What do you intend to do about…?
- Have you given any more thought to…?
- Are you intending on…?
- Have you made a decision about…?

### Asking for clarification
- I'm sorry, but I didn't catch that…
- Would you mind repeating that for me?
- Could you say that one more time?
- You're saying that…?

**Let's Practice**
» Planning an overseas business trip
» Obtaining an address
» Speaking with a poor telephone connection

# Simulation 2

## Case Study (Group)

### A. Background

Fairmont Industries is an international construction firm that is headquartered in the U.K. They supply teams of expert engineers and project managers to work on large-scale construction ventures around the world. Fairmont has recently entered into an agreement with Qatar Oil, Ltd. to construct a new refinery near Doha. Although the construction will take place in Qatar, the planning will be completed at Fairmont's headquarters before the engineering team is sent to Doha to collaborate with local contractors.

### B. Task

The engineering team at Fairmont is beginning to establish a relationship with the local contractors. Planning is still in the preliminary stage with British and Qatari teams working on separate ends of the project. As plans for the project are developing, it has become necessary for the respective teams to begin collaborating on several key issues. This conference call is one of the few times all parties are coming together and introductions are necessary to help the smooth flow of the meeting.

**In this meeting, they aim to:**
- Set a date for the U.K. engineering team and project leaders to visit the local site together.
- Establish a time frame for the completion of the project.
- Discuss budget issues.

### C. Roles

**FORMAL vs. INFORMAL** — How would a formal meeting be different to an informal meeting in this scenario?

**Participant A: Fairmont Doha Project Leader**
- ✓ Hopes to visit the construction site in September or early October.
- ✓ Aims to have the project completed by June.
- ✓ Has been ordered by Fairmont to reduce costs by 5%.

**Participant B: Fairmont Project Engineer**
- ✓ Is available to visit the construction site any time.
- ✓ Believes the project can be completed in 8 months.
- ✓ Has been ordered by the company to do whatever is possible to reduce costs.

**Participant C: Qatar Construction Company Representative**
- ✓ Is involved in another project that will be completed at the end of September.
- ✓ Hopes to break ground on the Qatar Oil refinery by mid-October.
- ✓ Thinks the budget that has been set is unrealistic for the time frame and hopes to raise the operating budget by 7% in order to employ extra workers to finish by June.

# Effective Conference Call Checklist

## ✱ Meeting preparation
- Has a meeting time been set? ✓
- Have attendees been formally invited? ☐
- Did everyone RSVP or notify the organizers that they will be unable to attend? ☐
- Is everyone aware any special responsibilities that they have? ☐
- Are all parties aware of how and when to connect to the call? ☐

## ✱ Opening a meeting
- Have all parties been introduced through official greetings? ☐
- Has the purpose of the meeting reestablished? ☐
- Are all parties aware of their roles and responsibilities? ☐
- Has the agenda been reviewed? ☐

## ✱ Meeting procedure
- Did everyone join the call at the agreed upon time? ☐
- Was a moderator appointed? ☐
- Was the agenda made clear to participants? ☐
- Did everyone stay on topic? ☐

## ✱ Meeting follow-up
- Were all documents mentioned in the meeting shared? ☐
- Was anyone assigned any special tasks in the meeting? ☐
- Is a progress check necessary? ☐
- Was the next meeting scheduled? ☐
- Were there any connection issues that need to be resolved by the next meeting? ☐

## ✱ Effective meeting language
- Did each speaker state his or her name before beginning? ☐
- Did participants speak clearly and slowly? ☐
- Were attendees able to ask for clarification when necessary? ☐
- Did each speaker make his or her point understood? ☐

## ✱ Conference call tactics
- Were handouts sent prior to the call? ☐
- Was time used efficiently? ☐
- Were all members able to participate? ☐
- Were all participants located in areas with minimal background noise? ☐

### Tips!
- When making international conference calls, it is important to be aware of the international dateline and how it affects your appointment time.
- Minimize the language barrier by e-mailing relevant presentation notes and slides before the meeting. By allowing your listener to see what you will discuss in writing, you can reduce miscommunication.

**Chapter. 3**

# Meeting Procedures

One of the main purposes of a group meeting is to collaborate with others. For this reason, the time used to present ideas and hold discussion makes up a large part of an overall meeting. This chapter aims to provide you with the tools to stimulate and encourage constructive participation to get the most of each meeting. We will cover crucial meeting skills, including :

› Presenting ideas
› Participating in discussions
› Giving and responding to opinions
› Following meeting procedures

Look at the conversation between Faheem, Paul, and Linda. How do they address the key elements to collaborating with others during a meeting?
Compare the steps give above with the conversation for ideas on how to effectively discuss and share ideas during a meeting.

## Discussions and Ideas.

| | |
|---|---|
| Paul | **Right, I think that covers the first item.** Does anyone have anything to add? |
| Faheem | No, I think we're good. |
| Paul | Okay then, **the next item on the agenda is** to discuss the introduction of our Atemz Product into the Japanese market. Linda, **would you like to introduce this item?** |
| Linda | **Can I draw your attention to** the screen? These are the figures for the Atemz product's profits in the Chinese market. Now, considering that our Japanese branch has spent the last six months researching and preparing for new product launches, it has come to the attention of the International Product Marketing Department that now would be a good time. |
| Faheem | **I'm not sure what you mean by** integrating the success of the product in the Chinese market to our discussions about the product in Japan. |
| Linda | To put it simply, we can use the Chinese model to estimate and plan our marketing strategy for Atemz's launch in Japan. **Let me emphasize** that the similarities of the two markets have been considered in making these comparisons. |
| Faheem | Oh, how did we go about the research for this? |
| Paul | I think **we're missing the point** here. If I could add, **I agree, but** I'm still unsure whether this is good enough to push forward the product launch. |
| Linda | Well, **as I said earlier,** the timing for the launch has been examined by the International Product Marketing Department with cooperation from the Japanese branch. I think we should prepare in advance and find ways to support this launch. **Somebody mentioned** previous marketing plans? |
| Faheem | Ah, yes. **Have you considered** reviewing the marketing strategies used for Brenzil? I remember we were pretty successful with its launch in Japan. |
| Paul | **I'm 100% behind** Faheem on that. |

## useful expressions

The expressions below can be used to effectively participate in meeting discussions. Take the time to review the expressions and find them in the CASE "Discussions and Ideas."

1. Right, I think that covers the first item.
2. The next item on the agenda is...
3. Let me emphasize...
4. Have you considered...?
5. We're missing the point.
6. I'm not sure what you mean by...?
7. I agree, but...
8. I'm 100% behind...
9. ..., would you like to introduce this item?
10. As I said earlier...
11. Can I draw your attention to...?
12. Somebody mentioned...

## Language practice

Reword and write the sentences using the Useful Expressions.

1. **I'd like to point out** that we are already 2 weeks behind on this.

2. **As mentioned before,** it's important to get these dates fixed as soon as possible.

3. **I think we're getting off the point.** We should be discussing the need for a new marketing strategy, not the cause and effects of micro marketing.

4. **Let's move to the next item on the agenda,** this quarter's marketing quota.

5. **What about looking into** sharing the task with the production team?

6. **I'm not sure what you're getting at by** suggesting that we should change the designs.

7. **I'm not against** the idea of outsourcing, but I think it's not as simple as it sounds.

8. **Someone said something about** adjusting the production schedule. Could they go into more details?

9. **Can I get everyone to have a look at** the handouts?

10. **I entirely agree with you** on this proposal.

# How to

**Theoretically**

## Collaborate in a meeting

How should you collaborate in a meeting? It all comes down to participating in active discussion and listening. Unless the meeting's agenda is straightforward, a compromise must be reached to agree on most of the issues. Although it is difficult to consistently find a compromise that is reasonable to everyone, this is what all meetings should strive towards. In order for participants to understand the details of the agenda being discussed and effectively participate and share their opinions, a few areas need to be kept in mind.

What are the points you need to consider when looking at the three elements for collaborating in a meeting?
Discuss and share your ideas in groups.

### Presentation

A good presentation is often required for all participants to become up-to-date with the items on the agenda. A presentation should be used as a tool to help participants understand important matters easily and thus actively engage in discussions. Presenters should prepare all materials beforehand and, if required, use visuals aids or handouts to deliver key information.

### Active listening

For successful communication, it is important not only to have good delivery skills, but also to be an active listener. Active listeners:
- Receive the speaker's comprehensive message (verbal, visual, and non-verbal)
- Interpret the speaker's message as accurately as possible
- Check the interpreted message for accuracy by rephrasing it for the speaker

### Open-mindedness

Productive team discussions require participants to listen with open minds and respect the views of others. Open-minded participants try to reach a decision that benefits the group or company as a whole.

**Presentation**

**Active listening**

**Open-mindedness**

# MEETING SKILLS

## Presentations

**Exercise 1**

Many meetings require some form of presentation. To deliver an effective presentation there are many aspects to be considered. Think about the last time you presented at a meeting. What were some things you had to prepare beforehand? What made your presentation successful? And what could make it even better? Use the area below to brainstorm of the things that make presentations successful.

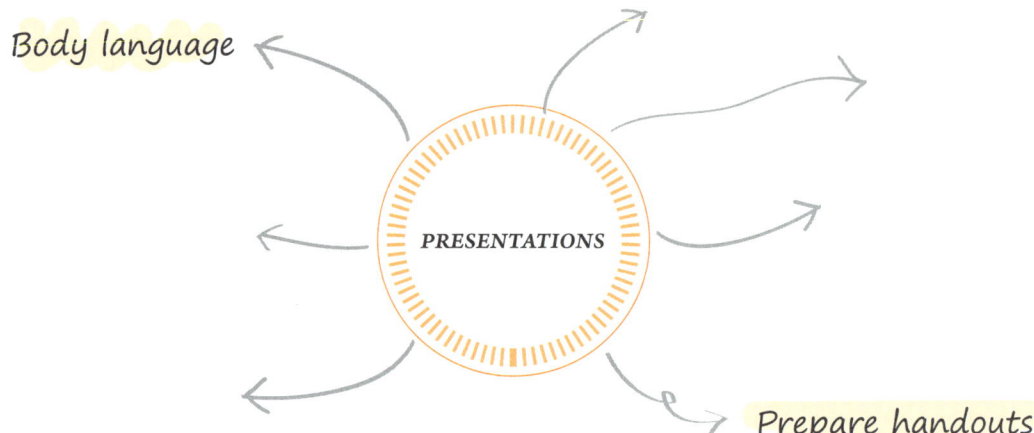

# MEETING SKILLS

## Discussions

**Exercise 2**

In a majority of meetings, attendees are expected to give their ideas and contribute their opinions about the item at hand. Take a look at the topics 1-4 below and share your opinion. In the space provided write down something you might say to a person who disagrees with you.

1. Using alternative energy to create a "green" company image at the cost of damaging short-term profits.

2. Adopting a flexible work hour scheme.

# Following Procedures

**Exercise 3**

Read the meeting objectives of each meeting set and review the list of items on each agenda. How would you order each item to make sure the meetings run efficiently?

## MEETING A

**Objective:** To review how working practices can be improved in the organization

- ____ Action plan
- ____ Review issues by department
- ____ Brainstorm solutions
- ____ Brainstorm blind spots or potential problems
- ____ Introduce each department and their roles

## MEETING B

**Objective:** To produce a list of potential names for a new product

- ____ Product features overview
- ____ Follow- up report
- ____ Brainstorm possible names
- ____ Target market review
- ____ Comparison to competitor's products

## MEETING C

**Objective:** To persuade a supplier to revise a contract

- ____ Current contract details
- ____ Q&A
- ____ Meeting purpose overview
- ____ Revise contract proposal
- ____ Explanation of mutual benefits from the contract revision

## MEETING D

**Objective:** HR meeting to consider updating the company dress code policy

- ____ Policy change process overview
- ____ Amendments to the proposal
- ____ Presentation of current and proposed dress code
- ____ Brainstorm and opinions
- ____ Action plan and follow-up list

---

**3** Extending paid maternity leave to 9 months and introducing a 6-month paid paternity leave option.

**4** Outsourcing the Customer Service Center to save costs but risk losing customer loyalty.

# Check List

## Presenting and discussions

Think about a meeting that you recently attended or a meeting that you have planned for the future. Use the checklist below to check off the essential aspects to presenting and participating in discussions during a meeting.

» How did you collaborate with others in the past?
» How do you plan on involving yourself at meetings in the future?

### • Presenting Ideas
- Were the presenters informed of the schedule and their responsibilities? ✓
- Were all participants aware of the presentation topic? ☐
- Was sufficient time allocated for the presentation? ☐
- Were all materials prepared beforehand? ☐
- Were visual aids or handouts needed? ☐
- Were all electronics and other tools tested in advance? ☐

### • Participating in Discussions
- Were all participants actively involved in the discussions? ☐
- Were all participants given the chance to state and respond to different opinions? ☐
- Did the chairperson or designated person effectively guide the discussions? ☐
- Was a conclusion reached before closing the discussion? ☐

### • Following Agendas
- Was the agenda followed as planned? ☐
- If there were any changes made during the meeting proceedings was a follow-up plan made? ☐
- Was each item opened and closed without going off track? ☐
- Did the presentations and discussion proceed to reach a conclusion for each item? ☐

*Meeting Procedures*

## Common MISTAKES!

Have you ever heard the phrase, "biting off more than you can chew"? Simply put, it means to take on more than one is capable of doing. This is a common mistake made during meetings where there is a lot to complete in a limited time frame. In such cases, the discussions are rushed and many key issues can be overlooked. Be sure to provide enough time for discussions and keep the meeting agenda realistic and simple.

# 03 Simulation ›››

## Annual general meetings

(or AGM) are yearly meetings that include official company representatives and members of the general public, such as shareholders. These meetings are usually mandatory, being required by law or formally included in a company's charter. An AGM performs an informative function by updating the shareholders on the company's new and old business. These meetings provide shareholders with the opportunity to review fiscal information and ask questions to the directors about the future direction of the business.

### Topics covered in a general meeting might including :

- ✓ Filling vacancies on the board of directors.
- ✓ Presenting results from the past year's business activities.
- ✓ Discussing the next year's proposed business plans.
- ✓ Going over a company's financial statements.
- ✓ Declaring dividends that will be paid to the investors.

## Good to Know

Here are some expressions that are useful when participating in an AGM.

### Offering an explanation

- I think...can be attributed to...
- It's possible that...
- The facts point to...
- It is more than likely that...
- A likely explanation is that...

### Summing up

- In conclusion...
- Just to recap...
- I'd like to go over the main points again.
- In summary...
- After reviewing all the evidence, ....
- To wrap things up, I think...

### Presenting visuals

- As you can see in the chart...
- Here you can see a comparison of...
- This figure refers to...
- You will note a strong upward trend...
- Let me draw your attention to...

### Let's Practice

» Going over quarterly data
» Presenting the end results of a project
» Rationalizing a decrease in sales

# Simulation.3

## Case Study (Group)

### A. Background

It is the end of April and Mulhouse and Reimes (M&R) is preparing for their AGM. Ordinarily, the company holds the meeting at the end of May, but due to a poor economic atmosphere, the company is currently operating at a slight loss. Mid-June, an acquisition will be completed that should reverse their poor financial situation. The company cannot mention the acquisition to share holders until it is complete and they fear presenting the current data as it stands will shake investor confidence.

### B. Task

The board needs to decide whether to hold the meeting in May as usual and disclose their financial problems or defer the meeting until the end of July when the positive effects of the acquisition can be seen. In order to make a good decision, both sides will be presenting their views on how the AGM should be organized. A decision will be made by all the members of the board through a majority vote system after the presentations are made.

### C. Roles

**FORMAL vs. INFORMAL** — How would a formal meeting be different to an informal meeting in this senario?

**Participant A : Board Member 1**
- ✓ Wants to defer the AGM.
- ✓ Worries publicizing the current situation will cause share prices to drop.
- ✓ Has confidence that the circumstances are only temporary.

**Participant B : Board Member 2**
- ✓ Wants to maintain the regular timing of the AGM.
- ✓ Hopes disclosing the problem will help preserve investors trust.
- ✓ Fears that the acquisition might not have the positive effect they hope.

# Effective AGM Checklist

## *Meeting preparation
- Was a meeting place and time set? ✓
- Were shareholders notified sufficiently in advance? ☐
- Was data from the past year gathered? ☐
- Have all topics to be covered been researched and prepared? ☐

## *Meeting procedure
- Was the agenda outlined at the start of the meeting? ☐
- Did speakers stay on topic? ☐
- Were participants assigned to chair and take minutes? ☐
- Was time given for questions from the audience? ☐

## *Meeting collaboration
- Have the presentations been well organized? ☐
- Are the presenters aware of the order of their presentation? ☐
- Are any presentation materials including handouts organized before the start of the meeting? ☐
- Are all participants actively listening throughout the presentation? ☐

## *Meeting follow-up
- Were all documents used made available for public viewing after the meeting? ☐
- Is any further research required? ☐
- Were all topics included in the agenda covered? ☐
- Was anyone elected to a new position? What changes will this cause? ☐
- Were the minutes and the committee's findings publicized? ☐

## *Effective meeting language
- Was positive language used to discuss results? ☐
- Were questions answered clearly and directly? ☐
- Did speakers seem well informed about the topics covered? ☐
- Were precise words used to describe situations? ☐

## *AGM tactics
- Were visual materials sufficiently utilized? ☐
- Was all data used up-to-date and clearly defined? ☐
- Were any results summed up efficiently in the minutes? ☐
- Does any official business need to be carried on to another meeting's agenda? ☐

## Tips!
- After October 2007, it became optional for private companies in the U.K. to hold AGMs, unless the company's articles of association include one.
- In general, a maximum of 15 months can elapse between two AGMs, and stockholders must receive at least 21 days of advance written notice.

**Chapter. 4**

# Meeting Communication

Once a meeting is underway, it is important to hear from other participants. Listening to the ideas of other participants might be just what you need to resolve a challenging issue. However, as meetings can get heated, it is crucial that participants recognize how to deal with too many or sometimes too few opinions and ideas. This chapter aims to provide you with the practice required to deal with such meeting challenges. We will cover meeting skills, including :

› Asking for clarification
› Asking for comments and contributions
› Responding to offers and suggestions
› Dealing with interruptions

Look at the conversation between Royce, Michelle, and Carla. How do they address the key elements to sharing opinions and making suggestions during a meeting?
Compare the steps give above with the conversation for ideas on how to contribute to a meeting.

»

## Opinions and Suggestions.

**Royce** — So, **what you're saying** is that we have been focusing too much on the big cities and our customers there?

**Michelle** — Exactly. Our research indicates that the rural market has been largely untapped. **In my opinion, we should** give our rural sales teams more opportunities to expand their customer base.

**Royce** — **I can see what you're getting at**, but I think it's too early to be making a decision like this.

**Michelle** — **I understand your concern**, but the facts we have in front of us clearly show our weakness in the rural market.

**Carla** — **I'm sorry to interrupt, but** what exactly do you mean by "more opportunities"? Haven't we already increased the rural sales team funding?

**Royce** — **That's a very good point.** Michelle, what do you think?

**Michelle** — It's true that we have increased funding, but if you look at the statistics, the increase was hardly enough to support new business or marketing.

**Carla** — What do you suggest?

**Michelle** — Well, I think funding is an issue but we also have to keep in mind that the rural sales team is covering a lot of territory. There needs to be some HR* support.

**Carla** — **Let's hear what** HR **has to say.**

**Royce** — **Could I make a suggestion?** I think HR support is another issue altogether. **I suggest we take that up at another meeting.** Let's get back to looking into our weakness in the rural market. **We haven't heard from** R&D* **yet.** Ted, do you have anything to add?

*__HR:__ *Human Resource Department*
*__R&D:__ *Research and Development Department*

## useful expressions

**Effective Meeting Skills**

The expressions below can be used to effectively express opinions during meetings. Take the time to review the expressions and find them in the CASE "Opinions and Suggestions."

1. I suggest we take that up at another meeting.
2. Could I make a suggestion?
3. I'm sorry to interrupt, but…
4. That's a very good point.
5. We haven't heard from … yet.
6. Let's hear what … has to say
7. I can see what you're getting at…
8. I understand your concern…
9. What do you think?
10. In my opinion we should…
11. What you're saying is…

44

## Language practice

Review the Useful Expressions and match the sentences with the appropriate response.

1. What about the European markets? Don't we need to readjust our marketing strategy for Europe, too?
2. Is there anything else we need to add to this project proposal?
3. The R&D department needs to get up to date before we can arrange a meeting with the clients.
4. Do you think that our US branches have enough support to work through this issue?
5. We need some more ideas on how to make this product more marketable.
6. I'm sorry to interrupt, but is this procedure really necessary? We only need to review the results of the survey.
7. We haven't heard from Sarah yet. Sarah, do you have anything to add?
8. What about the environmental consequences? I'm not sure this is a good idea.
9. Shouldn't we review last quarter's data too? I don't think we have enough information to go on from here.

a. What you're saying is that the R&D department isn't prepared to be involved right away.
b. I suggest we take that up at another meeting. It's a little off topic.
c. If you just let me finish, you'll know exactly what I am getting at.
d. Good question. Let's hear what the U.S. branch managers have to say.
e. No, I think you've covered everything.
f. I understand your concern, but I assure you that all the required environmental standards have been upheld.
g. In my opinion, we should reevaluate our target customers for this product.
h. Could I make a suggestion? I think we should add more details about the scope of the project.
i. That's a very good point. Let's prepare a report including last quarter's data for our next meeting.

# How to Contribute in a meeting

**Theoretically**

How should you contribute at a meeting? No matter who you are, attending and effectively contributing at meetings will be expected of you in the workplace. However, having a lot does not always count towards effectively contributing to the meeting. The following are some areas participants should keep in mind to effectively contribute to a meeting.

Chapter.4 Meeting Communication

**Group Application**

What are the points you need to consider when reviewing the three elements to contributing to a meeting?
Discuss and share your ideas in groups.

### Organize your thoughts

Thoughts and ideas that have been organized before being thrown out for all to hear make better meetings. Rambling, disorganized ideas increase the likelihood that the meeting will get sidetracked. Make sure you keep to stating one idea at a time. Even if you are bursting with good ideas and suggestions, present them one at a time and at a relevant time, and it will have a more positive impact on the meeting.

### Relevance and evidence matter

Before you make a comment, take the time to consider whether your input is relevant. Irrelevant comments very often distract the group. Also, remember that opinions are ubiquitous. Everyone has an opinion, but good decisions and solutions are backed by evidence. Use facts, statistics, and examples to strengthen your thoughts and ideas.

### Use questions to obtain information

Use a mix of open and closed questions to bring out the information that you require. Open questions allow deeper and lengthier responses. These should be used when asking for opinions and ideas. Closed questions are answered with a simple yes, or no. Be wise and use questions to bring out the desired responses from participants.

---

**Organize your thoughts**

**Relevance and evidence matter**

**Use questions to obtain information**

# MEETING SKILLS

## Clarifying

**Exercise 1**

Often in meetings, confusion and conflict arise when participants misinterpret each other. To make sure that the speakers ideas are correctly understood, many skilled business people use 'paraphrasing.' Simply put, the speaker's words are rephrased and the ideas reestablished. Practice paraphrasing the sentences below to double check their meaning.

1. Research has shown that for many years now transport planners in the UK have been demanding that motorists pay directly for the use of roads.

   ○ What you are saying is that ................................................................

2. I've been told by the finance department that the dramatic fall in share prices took even the experts by surprise.

   ○ Do you mean to say that ................................................................

3. The new product line launched last summer has already surpassed our sales target.

   ○ That means ................................................................

4. What worries me is that they have so far failed to improve the quality of work.

   ○ So what you want to say is ................................................................

5. There has been a decline in the sales figures for the last two quarters. For us to invest in a new market at this time would be a terrible mistake.

   ○ ................................................................

6. The subject of budget cuts is irrelevant to reviewing the productivity of the Indonesian branch and factory.

   ○ ................................................................

# MEETING SKILLS

## Comments and Contributions

**Exercise 2**

In a majority of meetings, attendees are expected to give their ideas and contribute their opinions.
However, just because participation is important, an untimely comment or irrelevant input is never for the best in business situations. Look at each situation. What would be the best thing to say or do?

### Scene 1.

You are a middle-level team leader. The AGM is to be held next month and team leaders have been called in to help divide the roles and responsibilities of each team for preparing the AGM. So far no one has volunteered for any role.

### Scene 2.

You are a plant manager. On short notice, a potential overseas buy has come in for a meeting. The client wishes to talk about writing up a contract and insists that a general draft is designed during the meeting. You and your sales team manager are not exactly sure what the client wants.

### Scene 3.

You are at a team meeting. Your team leader has come up with some ideas to deal with the problem of low overall team performance. Some of your team members disagree strongly with the rewards system that the team leader wants to try.

---

# MEETING SKILLS

## Handling Interruptions

**Exercise 3**

Interruptions are inevitable. Interruptions that are made at the right place at the right time can be helpful in keeping the discussion and meeting on track. However, not all interruptions are useful. Instead, they can be distracting and disengage meeting participants. When are interruptions appropriate? What are some ways to deal with inappropriate interruptions? Brainstorm and add to the categories below.

| Appropriate Interruptions | Inappropriate Interruptions | How to deal with Interruptions |
|---|---|---|
| • While brainstorming | • When you disagree with the speaker | • "If you don't mind, could I please finish first?" |
| • | • | • |
| • | • | • |
| • | • | • |
| • | • | • |
| • | • | • |

# Check List

## Opinions and Interruptions

Think about a meeting that you recently attended or a meeting that you have planned for the future. Use the checklist below to check off the essential aspects to handling different opinions and interruptions during a meeting.

» *How did you handle various types of contributions in the past?*
» *How do you plan on contributing to meetings in the future?*

### Clarifications

1. Were participants given time to paraphrase the main ideas? (✓)
2. Did speakers allow for questions to help all participants understand the main ideas? ( )
3. Were all participants asked if they understood clearly? ( )
4. Were any misunderstandings cleared up before moving on? ( )

### Comments, Contributions, and Suggestions

1. Were comments made at the correct time? ( )
2. Were ideas and thoughts thoroughly considered through before suggestions were made? ( )
3. Did all participants have the opportunity to contribute to the meeting? ( )
4. Were suggestions backed by facts and numbers not just opinions? ( )

### Interruptions

1. Were interruptions made in a timely manner? ( )
2. Were the interruptions dealt with so both parties shared their ideas? ( )
3. Did the designated meeting chair effectively cut out unhelpful comments and interruptions? ( )

## Common MISTAKES!

Enthusiastic participants are often bursting with good ideas and suggestions. However, they fall into the trap of presenting their ideas and thoughts as a string of irrelevant points. It's good to remember that fellow participants will be more likely to listen if you present them one at a time and at an appropriate time.

# Simulation 04

## Damage control meetings

**Damage control meetings** are the last chance to work out unresolved issues. Sometimes unforeseeable problems arise in business, and swift action is necessary to repair the situation. These meetings have an important role in maintaining good relations as they enable staff to troubleshoot problems and rectify unfortunate circumstances before they cause permanent harm to a working relationship.

**In damage control meetings, it is important to:**
- ✓ Think creatively to come up with solutions.
- ✓ Keep a calm head.
- ✓ Act sincerely and be on one's best behavior.
- ✓ Be ready to compromise and offer compensation.
- ✓ Come prepared with a full understanding of the issue that needs to be discussed.

**Here are some expressions that are useful when holding damage control meetings.**

### Offering advice
- Have you considered…?
- Why don't you try…?
- If I were in your situation, I would…
- You should try to…
- I'd be happy to…

### Reassuring someone
- I can assure you that…
- I guarantee that we will do all that we can to…
- Despite what you may have heard…
- Rest assured that…
- This situation is under control.

### Offering an apology
- Will you forgive me for…?
- I should apologize for…
- I have to take the blame for…
- I'm sorry, but I should have…
- …was completely my fault.

**Let's Practice**
» Discussing billing mistakes
» Discounting damaged products
» Explaining a missed deadline

# Simulation.4

## Group Case Study

### A. Background

Masuka Industrials designs and produces industrial equipment for manufacturing electronics. The company has an excellent reputation in the industry and prides itself both on the high quality of its products and on its customer satisfaction rate. Nearly 80% of Masuka's business comes from repeat customers and servicing contracts for equipment it has sold, so preserving the company's good name is essential in maintaining its success.

### B. Task

Through customer complaints, the company has become aware of an engineering flaw in the new generation of a piece of equipment that manufactures components for flat screen televisions. The defect causes between 13% and 17% of products produced using the machines to overheat when used for extended periods of time. The PR team has been tasked with coming up with an appropriate and cost-effective solution to the problem.

### C. Roles

**FORMAL vs. INFORMAL** How would a formal meeting be different to an informal meeting in this senario?

**Participant A:**
Masuka PR Team Member 1

- ✓ Favors a total product recall and replacement (would result in $3 million in losses).
- ✓ Wants to notify all purchasers of the problem.
- ✓ Fears waiting for customers to discover the problem on their own will harm the brand image.

**Participant B:**
Masuka PR Team Member 2

- ✓ Wants to avoid an expensive recall.
- ✓ Supports offering repair services on an as-needed basis (would result in $1.5 million in losses).
- ✓ Thinks disclosing the flaw could mean bad publicity.

# " Effective Damage Control Checklist "

### ✱ Meeting preparation
- Was a meeting time and place set in advance? ✓
- Was a clear agenda set? Were participants notified in advance? ☐
- What is the objective of the meeting? ☐
- Will the participants have special responsibilities? ☐

### ✱ Meeting procedure
- Who chaired the meeting? ☐
- Was someone tasked with recording minutes? ☐
- Was the agenda set at the start of the meeting? ☐
- Was the agenda followed? ☐

### ✱ Meeting follow-up
- Was the desired outcome achieved? ☐ If not, what will the next step be? ☐
- Was a deadline established for any tasks assigned? ☐
- Is a follow-up meeting necessary? ☐
- Was there anything that could be improved on before the next meeting? ☐

### ✱ Damage control meeting tactics
- Were you able to keep a calm and creative outlook? ☐
- Was there sufficient time to explore each topic? ☐
- Should anything be added to the next meeting's agenda? ☐
- Was time spent evaluating ideas and finding solutions? ☐

### ✱ Meeting contributions
- Were the ideas presented in an organized fashion? ☐
- Were the contributions relevant to the topic? ☐
- Were ideas supported by facts and examples? ☐
- Were questions used to obtain information? ☐

### ✱ Effective meeting language
- Were clear suggestions offered to participants? ☐
- Was all criticism constructive? ☐
- Did all attendees receive a chance to talk? ☐
- Was positive participation encouraged? ☐
- Did speakers stay on topic? ☐

---

## Tips!

- "I'm sorry" doesn't always translate. Americans are likely to see an apology as admitting some wrongdoing on the apologizer's part whereas Japanese are likely to issue an apology in cases where they are not responsible simply to express that a situation is unfortunate.

- In Japanese business culture, good manners are essential. The Japanese tend to try to avoid conflict and unpleasant feelings. For this reason, avoid saying no if possible. Instead, hedge your rejection by making statements like, "This might be too challenging," to allow partners to save face.

Chapter. 5

# Closing Meetings

The end of a meeting is just as important as the actual meeting itself. This is your last chance to make sure that all objectives are achieved and that all issues are dealt with. This chapter aims to give you the skills you need to make sure that your meeting ends on a successful note. We will look at key aspects that need to be considered when closing a meeting, such as:

› Summarizing the proceedings
› Reaching a consensus on issues from the meeting
› Evaluating the meeting
› Organizing action plans for meeting follow-up

Look at the conversation between Angela, Tom, and Marcus. How do they address the key elements to effectively ending a meeting?
Compare the steps give above with the conversation for ideas on how to end a meeting.

# CASE

## Wrapping Up.

**Angela** — We are **running short on time** so **let's wrap up our discussions.** Tom?

**Tom** — Yes, **just to quickly recap,** we should set up a committee to deal with the payment problems that customers have been reporting.

**Marcus** — I think that **we've basically all agreed that** this is necessary. I suggest we put it to a vote and finalize things.

**Angela** — That's a good idea. **Can you give me a show of hands** about the issue? All those in favor? All opposed?

**Marcus** — Great, it's unanimous. We need to work out who will head this committee.

**Angela** — Sorry, **if no one objects, can we come back to** this issue next week?

**Tom** — Yes, let's stop here. Now **to summarize our decisions**, we all agreed that the payment system needs to be improved, and a committee will be put together to oversee the execution of improvement plans.

**Angela** — Now, **is there anything under AOB*?**

**Marcus** — No, I think that's everything.

**Angela** — Okay. **I'm going to** put forward an agenda for our next meeting. It should be in your inbox by Wednesday at the latest and Jenny will pass on the minutes. **Thank you for your attention**. We really got through a lot today.

**Tom** — I agree, definitely by far the most productive meeting we've had in a while. **Thanks for coming in.** I'll see you all next week.

*****AOB:** Any Other Business

# useful expressions

The expressions below can be used to effectively close a meeting. Take the time to review the expressions and find them in the CASE "Wrapping Up."

**Effective Meeting Skills**

1. ... running short on time.
2. Let's wrap up our discussions.
3. Just to quickly recap...
4. We've basically all agreed that...
5. Can you give me a show of hands...
6. If no one objects, can we come back to...
7. To summarize our decisions...
8. Is there anything under AOB?
9. I'm going to...
10. Thank you for your attention.
11. Thanks for coming in.

54

# Language practice

**Review the Useful Expressions and put the sentences in the correct order.**

**A**
___ Yes, I think that would be for the best.
___ If no one objects, can we come back to this issue next meeting?
___ I think we're running short on time.

**B**
___ Earlier, we mentioned that the marketing team needs to be informed of the new changes.
___ Is there anything under AOB?
___ Yes, we need to work on getting the marketing team involved.

**C**
___ So, just to quickly recap, we are going ahead with the new project as planned.
___ Wonderful. Thanks for coming in, everyone.
___ Great. I'm going to send everyone the meeting minutes with the action plan and R&R outlined in more details.

**D**
___ Okay then, let's wrap up our discussions. Mark, can you quickly go over the notes?
___ Yes, to summarize our decisions, we have decided against attending the conference in Florida due to schedule conflicts, but we will schedule a meeting with the US R&D team for next month.
___ James, I think we might have to cut it here.

**E**
___ Can you give me a show of hands? So, it's unanimous then.
___ Okay, now let's move on.
___ We've basically all agreed that we want to have Tom take his place as the TF leader.

# How to

### Theoretically

## Close a meeting

Just as starting a meeting on a positive note is important; a positive finish to a meeting is something that all business people should aim for. How should you close a meeting? What should be done to ensure that the entire meeting is not in vain? As the participants of a meeting prepare to wrap up and gather their ideas, there are a few items that should be dealt with to make certain that the purpose of the meeting was reached.

**Group Application**

What are the points you need to consider when you are preparing the four elements for closing a meeting?
Discuss and share your ideas in groups.

### Summarize the proceedings

Very often, participants will complain about a meeting being a complete waste of time. This is usually because the results of the meeting are not defined clearly. Make sure that time is set aside to review the proceedings of the meeting and go over what was or wasn't achieved.

### Reach a consensus

Before the meeting is over, it is important that participants reach a consensus on the issues that were handled in the meeting. Making sure that everyone is on the same page is crucial for productive meetings and also for productive follow-up.

### Evaluate the meeting

Make sure to leave some time to evaluate the meeting. Was it productive? Were all the items on the agenda discussed? Was there enough time? Only after evaluations can the meeting be improved and the necessary follow-up steps taken.

### Organize follow-up

The meeting does not simply end when the time is up. Before closing a meeting, the actions that need to be taken to follow-up on the meeting should be established clearly to prevent any confusion among participants.

---

**Summarize the proceedings**

**Reach a consensus**

**Evaluate the meeting**

**Organize follow-up**

# MEETING SKILLS

## Summarizing the discussion

**Exercise 1**

Different people have different understandings and memories of what took place and what was agreed upon. Therefore, it is a good idea to make sure all participants leave the meeting with a common understanding of the meetings proceedings and results to avoid future problems. Look at the meeting agendas below and create possible meeting summaries.

### Meeting Agenda

**A Purpose:** To review the feasibility of implementing joint-venture marketing of the online training program.

**Item 1:** Consider need to develop a marketing strategy.
**Item 2:** Brainstorm information needed to be shared for a joint-venture.
**Item 3:** TF action plan for technical and non-technical tasks.

**B Purpose:** To plan the promotion of a new product.

**Item 1:** Consider initial trials in major cities.
**Item 2:** Compare in-store promotions to online or other media-based promotions.
**Item 3:** Schedule feedback for the promotion results.

**C Purpose:** To discuss proposals for increasing our warehouse capacity.

**Item 1:** Current warehouse situation review.
**Item 2:** Brainstorm different options and compare pros/cons.
**Item 3:** Draft up proposal and create an action plan.

**D Purpose:** To negotiate final terms of contract for new product with client.

**Item 1:** Review last year's prices and terms.
**Item 2:** Negotiation contract for product price and contract period.
**Item 3:** Agree on the follow-up plans with the client.

### Possible Meeting Summary

**A**

**B**

**C**

**D**

**Reaching a consensus**

**Exercise 2**

What are some ways to reach a consensus? Depending of various situations, there are different ways to arrive at an agreement. Look at the following tools. How are they used to reach a consensus? What are their strengths and weaknesses? In what situations are they suitable to be used? Can you think of any other methods?

- Anonymous vote
- Show of hands
- Debate
- Presentation

**Evaluating the Meeting**

**Exercise 3**

Evaluating the meeting can help participants determine whether the meeting was successful and reached its goals. Using a checklist can help with this process. Look at the list of questions provided. How can these questions be useful in evaluating the meeting? Can you think of any other questions?

**How is this question useful?**

- Did the meeting start and end on time? →
- Were discussions unfocused? →
- Did people have the opportunity to add to the agenda? →
- Was the logistics appropriate and helpful? →
- Were issues thoughtfully reviewed or was the decision rushed? →
- Was too much time spent talking about issues rather than making decisions? →
- What decisions were made at the meeting and whose work or interests do they affect? →
- Did any one person dominate the discussion? →
- Was the chair's or president's facilitation of the meeting smooth and constructive? →
- What was the best thing about the meeting? →
- What should be repeated, and what should be improved? →
- →
- →

# Check List

## Closing a meeting

Think about a meeting that you recently attended or a meeting that you have planned for the future. Use the checklist below to check off the essential aspects to closing a meeting.

» How did you end meetings in the past?
» How do you plan on ending meetings in the future?

### Summarizing the Proceedings

- Were the outcomes shared? ✓
- Do all participants have a common understanding of the meeting results? ____
- Were any misunderstandings handled before the meeting ended? ____

### Reaching a Consensus

- Was a consensus reached on all items on the agenda? ____
- Were all participants involved in reaching a consensus? ____
- Will any issues or following agendas be dealt with? ____

### Evaluating the Meeting

- Was the outcome of the meeting compared to the original goal? ____
- Did participants make an input on their opinions of the meeting proceedings? ____
- Were suggestions made on how to make the next meeting better? ____

### Organizing Action Plans

- Was an action plan made? ____
- Do the necessary people know of the action plan's details? ____
- Do all participants know what to expect after the meeting? ____

*Closing a meeting*

## Common MISTAKES!

Many meeting leaders fail to sum up the main points at the end of the meeting. This can leave participants feeling unsure of what was accomplished. Even if a consensus was not reached on an issue, it is useful to quickly sum up what was talked about and outline what needs to be continued at the next meeting.

# 05 Simulation ›››

## Progress report meetings

are critical in keeping the development of a project on schedule. These internal meetings are a time for introspection and assessment of what has been done and what needs to be. By meeting at regular intervals to evaluate progress, it is possible to get the necessary feedback solve problems promptly and avoid wasting company resources.

### In order for a progress report meeting to go smoothly, participants must :

- ✓ Bring any relevant evidence to show what they have done since the last meeting.
- ✓ Come prepared to speak about the current state of their work.
- ✓ Think critically to make suggestions about how others could improve their work.
- ✓ Be able to confidently discuss their progress in relation to the expectations that were established in previous meetings.

## Good to Know

Here are some expressions that are useful when participating in a progress report meeting.

### Requesting feedback

- What are your thoughts on…?
- Would you mind looking over this for me?
- I'd like to get your opinion on…
- If you have a suggestion, I'd love to hear it.
- I'd be interested in hearing what you think about…

### Offering criticism

- I think it would be better if you…
- … needs additional consideration.
- I can foresee difficulties with…
- I'm not sure … would work, because…
- I've noticed that…

### Offering a compliment

- I'm impressed with the way you…
- You handled … really well.
- I have to compliment you on…
- Your … is admirable.

### Let's Practice

» **Troubleshooting a project problem**
» **Asking a supervisor for advice**
» **Reassuring a co-worker about an issue**

# Simulation.5

*Effective Meeting Skills*

## Group Case Study

### A Background

Evermore Productions has begun developing a new sequel in their successful action movie franchise, Free Fall. In order to make the next film more appealing to an international audience, the company has assigned a team to do market research into previously unsuccessful demographics. The past few releases in the series have performed well in the U.S. and other Western countries, but they have done poorly in other more conservative marketplaces, in particular, the Middle East.

### B Task

The Evermore production team is meeting to get an update from team members who have been collaborating with a consumer research team in Dubai. They plan to discuss the team's preliminary findings and decide which issues need more research and what to focus on as they continue with project development. It is crucial that a summary the meeting proceedings and a follow-up list are created at the closing of the meeting

### C Roles

  How would a formal meeting be different to an informal meeting in this senario?

**Participant A : Evermore Project Developer**

- ✓ Wants to know what changes will make the movie more marketable.
- ✓ Hopes to find out which demographics need additional focus grouping.
- ✓ Is open to suggestions, but feels too much change could alienate their current audience.

**Participant B : Evermore Research Leader**

- ✓ Suggests removing overt sexual references to reduce editing for Muslim audiences.
- ✓ Wants to change the film to make it more appealing to female audiences.
- ✓ Would like to eliminate Middle Eastern villain to improve movie publicity.

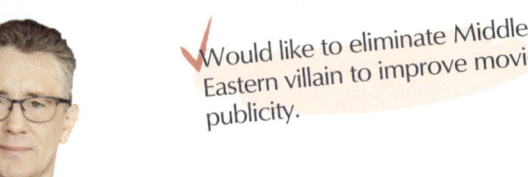

# "Effective Progress Report Checklist"

**Tips!**
- In Middle Eastern countries, meetings do not often follow a linear flow. They may not be structured with an agenda or targets in mind.
- Meeting times should always be confirmed verbally a few days in advance. Avoid scheduling appointments too far in advance as personal situations might change.

## ✱ Meeting preparation
- Was a meeting time and place been set? ✓
- Have attendees been invited? ☐
- Did everyone RSVP or notify the organizers that they will be unable to attend? ☐
- Is everyone aware of any special responsibilities that they will have? ☐
- Have all necessary documents and equipment been prepared in advance? ☐

## ✱ Meeting procedure
- Was there any unfinished business? If so, is there a plan to address it? ☐
- Were all agenda topics covered? ☐
- Was time given to discuss each point? ☐
- Do any files from the meeting need to be shared? ☐

## ✱ Closing a meeting
- Were the meeting's proceeding's summarized? ☐
- Was a consensus reached? ☐
- Was the meeting evaluated? ☐
- Was a follow up plan discussed? ☐

## ✱ Meeting follow-up
- Was there any unfinished business? If so, is there a plan to address it? ☐
- Has a plan been made for the next meeting? ☐
- Were roles assigned in the action plans? ☐
- Will the minutes be distributed? If so, to whom? ☐

## ✱ Effective meeting language
- Was sufficient detail used in updates? ☐
- Did any points require further clarification? ☐
- Was enough time given for follow-up questions? ☐
- Were minority views heard? ☐

## ✱ Progress report meeting tactics
- Did participants bring relevant documents to demonstrate their progress? ☐
- Did everyone get a chance to speak and receive feedback? ☐
- Have clear goals been set for what needs to be done before the next meeting? ☐
- Have plans been made to deal with any problems that were revealed? ☐

**Chapter. 6**

# Meeting Follow-up

An effective meeting continues after it is over through meeting follow-up. Following up on a meeting is crucial in making sure that the outcomes are reached. Quickly and accurately following up on a meeting maintains the energy created during the meeting and drives to accomplish the goals stated during the meeting. Generating meeting minutes is a simple tool used by successful business people. This chapter aims to give you the skills you need to ensure that meetings are correctly followed up upon. We will look at key aspects that need to be considered when following up on a meeting, such as :

› Writing meeting minutes
› Sharing meeting minutes
› Checking action plans

Look at the conversation between Angela, Tom, and Marcus. How do they address the key elements to effectively ending a meeting?
Compare the steps give above with the conversation for ideas on how to end a meeting.

>>>

## Follow-up.

**Jake** — Christine, sorry do you have a minute? There is something I need to ask.

**Christine** — Is this about the meeting we had this morning?

**Jake** — Yeah. **I was designated to** write up the meeting minutes and send out the reports collected during the meeting by this afternoon. But I just wanted to **check something with** you first before sending it out.

**Christine** — Oh, I see. Look, if you weren't sure about something, you should have said something during the meeting.

**Jake** — I know. I should have cleared it up. I'm sorry.

**Christine** — There's no need to apologize. Just make sure you speak up next time, okay? Now, what did you need me to look at?

**Jake** — Could you look over the notes, just to make sure I didn't miss anything? And I also have a **few details that need to be confirmed**.

**Christine** — Okay, I'm listening. Can you go over what you've got?

**Jake** — At 12 o'clock, the chair called the meeting to order, and I conducted a roll call. All members were in attendance. Then, the chair outlined the agenda, and old business was discussed. We voted on going forward with the Bayridge Condominiums project with a show of hands. The motion passed 7 to 2. Sally Roberts was tasked with contacting contractors, and Harry Olsen **was assigned to keep the team updated on** the project. We moved on to new business and discussed preparations for the upcoming industry conference. The chair moved to close the meeting. **Does anything else need to be added?**

**Christine** — Okay, a few things need to be added. **Make a note that** the Bayridge Condominiums report **needs to be shared by** next Thursday.

**Jake** — Yes, I'll put that in. One other thing, **could you repeat** the names of the contractors we agreed on?

**Christine** — Let me just look at my notes. Okay, Austin Industries, Williams Brothers Construction, and Manhattan Construction Company were mentioned. Any more questions?

**Jake** — No, that's it. Thank you. I'll remember to speak up next time.

**Christine** — Sure, no worries. Remember to **send out the e-mail before** 4p.m., and **be sure to include** Patrick.

## useful expressions

The expressions below can be used to effectively close a meeting. Take the time to review the expressions and find them in the CASE "Follow-up."

1. ... was designated to...
2. ... few details that need to be confirmed.
3. Be sure to include...
4. Send out the e-mail before...
5. Could you repeat...?
6. ... needs to be shared by...
7. Make a note that...
8. Does anything else need to be added?
9. ... was assigned to...
10. Keep the team updated on...
11. Check something with...

## Language practice

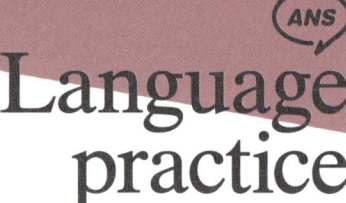

**Respond to the questions using the Useful Expressions.**

1. Who is responsible for sending out the sales reports?
   ...............................................................................................

2. Can you recall the dates for the international design convention?
   ...............................................................................................

3. Could you make sure the team knows what's happening with the Maddison project?
   ...............................................................................................

4. When do you plan on sending out the e-mail? Is everything ready?
   ...............................................................................................

5. I think I've got everything down. Does anything else need to be added?
   ...............................................................................................

6. Can each person go over their responsibilities just to clarify things?
   ...............................................................................................

7. What time do the contractors want the contract details by?
   ...............................................................................................

8. If everyone got that down, shall we move on?
   ...............................................................................................

9. I'm sorry could you remind me when the report should be sent out by?
   ...............................................................................................

# How to

## Theoretically

### Follow-up on a meeting

It is important to remember that a meeting does not simply end when the participants leave the room. Following up on a meeting is a key step in making sure that the time and resources put into the meeting do not go to waste. Generally speaking, the first step to following up on a meeting includes writing and sharing the meeting minutes. This way, a shared action plan is re-established, and the participants are reminded of their roles. There a few steps that should be kept in mind to effectively write and share meeting minutes.

**Importance of meeting minutes :**

Minutes are a tangible record of the meeting for its participants and a source of information for members who were unable to attend. Meeting minutes serve as a reference point for things and also can help notify individuals of tasks assigned to them and important timelines.

**Pre-planning meeting minutes :**

Before starting a meeting, if you are aware that you have been designated to write the minutes, prepare a suitable template or document format. At the very least, be sure to have a copy of the meeting agenda for reference, a list of all attendees, and all documents that are to be used during the meeting.

**Making notes :**

Before taking notes, it's important to understand the type of information that needs to be recorded at a meeting. Generally, minutes include the following: Date and time, a list of attendees, amendments to previous meeting minutes, decisions made for each agenda item, and action plans.

**Writing the minutes :**

Once the meeting is over, your notes should be organized and written up as a final copy of the meeting minutes. Be sure to write the minutes as soon as possible while everything is still fresh in your mind.

**Sharing meeting minutes :**

Finally, be sure to share the meeting minutes with the necessary people via the method stated during the meeting.

**Group Application**

What are the points you need to consider when you reviewing the five elements to following up on a meeting?
Discuss and share your ideas in groups.

**Importance of meeting minutes :**

**Pre-planning meeting minutes :**

**Making notes :**

**Writing the minutes :**

**Sharing meeting minutes :**

# MEETING SKILLS

## Writing Meeting Minutes

**Exercise 1**

In most cases, writing up meeting minutes can mean adding details to the meeting agenda determined at the start of a meeting. Work in groups to read the following example of a meeting agenda. Then, complete the meeting minutes in the area provided.

**Purpose** Plan the promotion of a new product.
**Item 1** Consider initial trials in major cities.
**Item 2** Compare in-store promotions to online or other media based promotions.
**Item 3** Schedule feedbacks for the promotion results.

Title _____ Date _____

Present

Apologies

Welcome

Meeting Purpose

**Exercise 2**

## Meeting Minutes Do's & Don'ts

Meeting minutes, like any other business report, should be written to accurately and efficiently share information. Read the tips and categorize them under the correct heading. Can you add any more?

### TIPS!

- Be concise. All you are required to do is to convey the essence of the meeting to its attendees and non-attendees in a brief format.
- Describe emotions of the attendees. Meeting minutes are supposed to be a concise and accurate document that refers only to business.
- Include any personal opinions about the happenings in the meeting.
- Spell out acronyms and abbreviations, at least when you use them for the first time in the text.
- Be specific. Otherwise, it will be difficult for the readers of your meeting minutes to understand the circumstances that led to the decision.
- Report on every little detail in your meeting minutes.
- Use bulleted lists when specifying comments, suggestions or decisions made.

**Exercise 3**

## Sharing Meeting Minutes

What are some ways to share meeting minutes? Depending of various situations, there are different ways to distribute meeting minutes. Look at the following tools, how are they used? What are their strengths and weaknesses? What situation are they suitable to be used? Can you think of any other methods?

# Check List

## Following up on a meeting

Think about a meeting that you recently attended or a meeting that you have planned for the future. Use the checklist below to check off the essential aspects to following up on a meeting.

» How did you follow-up on meetings in the past?
» How do you plan on following up on meetings in the future?

### Writing Meeting Minutes

- Were the minutes written up as soon as possible. ✓
- Were the minutes written in a pre-determined format?
- Do all participants have a common understanding of meeting minutes?
- Were any misunderstandings cleared up before sharing?

### Meeting Minutes Do's & Don'ts

- Were the minutes written appropriately?
- Were the minutes arranged to be simple, clear, and precise in communicating information and details?
- Were the minutes reviewed for any language errors?
- Were the meeting minutes concise?

### Sharing Meeting Minutes

- Were the outcomes shared?
- Were the minutes reviewed for any errors before being shared?
- Are all participants aware of how the minutes will be shared and by what deadline?

Meeting follow-up

## Common MISTAKES!

Often people need a gentle nudge to remind them about completing action items. Leaders need to check and ensure that actions are taking place as agreed. The check can be as simple as a short e-mail or phone call to those responsible. In some cases, not checking may send a message implying that follow-up is not necessary or important.

# Simulation 06

## Project initiation meetings

are internal meetings that set the stage for an upcoming project and its ultimate success or failure. A well-organized meeting provides a firm foundation for project development while a weak start could lead to sloppy work and troublesome issues later on. These meetings serve an essential purpose by helping participants understand the requirements and expectations of a project in addition to assigning tasks that need to be completed.

**Participants should come away from the meeting with:**

- ✓ An understanding of the scope of work of the project.
- ✓ Basic knowledge of any potential risks and issues associated with the project.
- ✓ Contact information for any outside participants who will be involved in the project.
- ✓ Details about the product timeline and requirements.
- ✓ An idea about the key milestones of the project.
- ✓ A plan for what their next step will be.

**Here are some expressions that are useful when holding project initiation meetings.**

### Welcoming a visitor
- I was happy to hear that you...
- I want to congratulate you on...
- It's nice to see you again.

### Offering new information
- I just want to update you on...
- The latest report indicates...
- It has recently been revealed that...
- To keep you apprised of the situation...
- I just want to bring you up to date on...

### Asking for elaboration
- Could you expound on...?
- What else can you tell us about...?
- Could you elaborate on...?
- Is there anything else you can tell us?
- Could you tell me a little more about...?
- Could you go into more detail?

**Let's Practice**

» Meeting with a potential business partner
» Discussing preliminary reports
» Organizing teams for a big project

# Simulation.6

## Case Study (Group)

### A. Background

Hotel La Cep is one of the premier resorts on France's southern coast. It is located on a historic seafront property and is a favorite among affluent tourists who summer in the area. The hotel has a well-established brand image and is overall happy with their status and clientele. It has been ten years since the hotel was last remodeled, and some areas of the hotel have begun to look dated.

### B. Task

A representative from Bayeux Design is coming to do a preliminary meeting with Hotel La Cep's general manager regarding the remodeling of the hotel. This would be the company's largest renovation project to date and they are eager to make a good impression. In order to make sure that the meeting does not go to waste, both parties must be aware of the roles and responsibilities especially in regards to post-meeting actions.

**Today, they will discuss:**
- The timeframe of the project.
- Their general vision for the hotel.

### C. Roles

**FORMAL vs. INFORMAL** — How would a formal meeting be different to an informal meeting in this scenario?

#### Participant A: Hotel La Cep General Manager

- ✓ Hopes the design consultant will spend some time at the hotel and get a sense of the clients.
- ✓ Wants to maintain a luxurious experience consistent with the brand image while incorporating new technology in the rooms.
- ✓ Needs to make sure that the work will not interrupt the high tourist season (June-August).

#### Participant B: Bayeux Design Consultant

- ✓ Already has a vision for the project and would like to get started as soon as possible.
- ✓ Wants to make a good impression on the hotel manager and establish a personal connection.
- ✓ Hopes to make extensive changes that may take more time than initially expected.

# Effective Project Initiation Checklist

## ✶ Meeting preparation
- Were a meeting time and place set? ✓
- Were attendees invited? ☐
- Did everyone RSVP or notify the organizers that they will be unable to attend? ☐
- Were attendees notified of any special responsibilities that they have? ☐
- Were all necessary documents and equipment prepared in advance? ☐

## ✶ Meeting procedure
- Was there an icebreaker or a warm-up activity? ☐
- Was someone tasked with recording minutes? ☐
- Was the purpose of the meeting clarified? ☐
- Did participants stick to the agenda? ☐

## ✶ Meeting follow-up
- Was there any unfinished business? If so, is there a plan to address it? ☐
- Has a plan been made for the next meeting? ☐
- Were roles assigned in the action plans? ☐

## ✶ Meeting minutes
- Was a format for the meeting minutes decided before the start of the meeting? ☐
- Was there a designated scribe for the meeting minutes? ☐
- Will the minutes be distributed? If so, to whom? ☐
- Do any files from the meeting need to be shared? ☐

## ✶ Effective meeting language
- Were minority views heard? ☐
- Were conflicts dealt with appropriately? ☐
- Was time spent evaluating ideas and finding solutions? ☐
- Did participants speak calmly and positively? ☐

## ✶ Project initiation meeting tactics
- Did participants stay on topic? ☐
- Was there sufficient time to cover each topic? ☐
- Have plans been made to deal with any problems the opinions highlighted? ☐
- Was everyone given a clear idea of what to do after the meeting? ☐

### Tips!
- In France, a small present is traditionally given at the beginning of a business relationship. This small gesture is necessary to start a negotiations on the right foot.
- The French respect privacy and a distinction between business and private matters. In order to establish a good business relationship, personal relationships must be established before business ones can be.

**Chapter. 7**

# Roles and Responsibilities

## Have you ever...

Have you ever been called into a meeting at the last minute with no clue as to what the agenda is or the meeting's purpose, let alone why you are there? Unfortunately, this isn't a rare phenomenon. Nearly every office worker experiences this at least once during his or her career. When you find yourself unprepared in a situation like this, it takes quick thinking and good improvisation skills to pull off a successful meeting.

Group

**Look at the statements below and discuss how you would act in each situation.**

1. You have suddenly been asked to participate in a meeting on behalf of a team member.

2. You have been chosen at random to chair a meeting because the regular chair is absent.

3. You are visiting a client's company for a monthly meeting; however, the host seems to have forgotten your appointment and is not prepared to receive you.

4. Your company is hosting an international conference on marketing strategies, and a company you were not expecting to participate has arrived from Vietnam.

5. Your team leader is running late to a 9 AM client meeting. He has asked you to delay the start.

## A gentleman says
Look at the expressions. How do they differ?

| GENERAL LANGUAGE | GENTLEMAN |
|---|---|
| 1. Let's get down to business. | → Shall we begin? |
| 2. I'd like to start by thanking everyone for coming out. | → First, I'd like to welcome our guests. |
| 3. Go ahead, Mark. | → Would you mind starting now, Mark? |
| 4. How about taking a break now? | → Should we pause for an intermission? |
| 5. Did everyone get one? | → Has everyone received a copy of the agenda? |
| 6. We're behind schedule. | → We're running a little short on time now. |
| 7. What do you have to say about that Mindy? | → Would you like to comment, Mindy? |

## Facilitating a meeting

**Exercise 1**

*What is it?*

Facilitating a meeting simply means to chair the meeting. You are responsible for organizing the flow of the meeting, managing agendas, greeting and introducing participants, and encouraging balanced participation among the attendees to bring about the desired results. An effective facilitator needs to promote a positive environment by maintaining an interested and enthusiastic demeanor.

## HOW TO...

**Rank the tasks that an effective facilitator completes in order of their importance to you.**

- (   ) Regulating the flow of discussion
- (   ) Asking open-ended questions to encourage conversation.
- (   ) Appointing someone to take minutes.
- (   ) Keeping conversations on track.
- (   ) Listening carefully to attendees' contributions.
- (   ) Having contributors clarify when things are unclear.
- (   ) Confirming details of the minutes.
- (   ) Maintaining polite and constructive conversation.
- (   ) Setting ground rules for the meeting.
- (   ) Trying to encourage collaboration instead of trying to persuade the group.

**Group — Partner work**

In pairs, write additional tasks of an effective facilitator and add to the list. Then share the results with the rest of the class.

☞ ..................................................................

☞ ..................................................................

☞ ..................................................................

☞ ..................................................................

☞ ..................................................................

# Host vs. Guest

### Exercise 2

It is common knowledge that an individual's behavior changes according to his or her role. In meetings the same principle applies. Guests and hosts are subject to certain obligations in regard to etiquette and protocol. In order to create an optimal environment for achieving an agenda, it is important that all parties adhere to their behavioral expectations.

**Host**
- ✓ Formalizing the agenda
- ✓ Providing directions and info to help guests prepare
- ✓ Arranging the meeting space
- Inviting attendees
- ✓ Guiding the meeting
- ✓ Ensuring that all attendees understand the meeting's objectives

**Guests**
- ✓ RSVP in advance to the meeting date
- ✓ Arriving at the scheduled time
- ✓ Confirming the meeting location
- ✓ Bringing along any necessary materials
- ✓ Listening politely to presentations
- ✓ Contributing positively

## HOW TO... (ANS)

**Read the list of responsibilities given below. Discuss and label whether each responsibility belongs to the Guest (G), Host (H), or Both (B).**

\_\_\_ Planning every detail ahead of time.
\_\_\_ Showing up at the agreed upon time.
\_\_\_ Bringing any necessary materials.
\_\_\_ Listening to presenters' contributions.
\_\_\_ Maintaining the flow of the meeting.
\_\_\_ Introducing attendees to one another.
\_\_\_ Writing and sharing the meeting minutes.
\_\_\_ Taking notes when necessary.
\_\_\_ Deciding on the structure of the meeting.
\_\_\_ Asking questions to further your understanding.

# Meeting DIY
## Roles and Responsibilities

Review the skills and ideas you have learned in this chapter that will help you to effectively lead or participate in meetings. Use the space provided below to create a personal action plan and set goals for meetings in the future.

## PERSONAL ACTION PLAN

| What I learned | Action |
|---|---|
|  |  |
| What I learned | Action |
|  |  |

## Meeting Skills TIP

**Don't ignore others' contributions.** – As participants make comments and ask questions during a meeting, quite often the reactions they receive will be used as a measure to how welcome their contributions are. Ignoring contributions will lead to less contributions being made.

# Simulation 07

## Brainstorming meetings

are internal meetings that aim to generate new ideas by encouraging an atmosphere where employees can speak freely. For these meetings, a creative mindset is essential. Attendees should be prepared to think quickly, share their thoughts about a specified topic, and both receive feedback about their contributions and give constructive input about teammates' ideas.

### Essentials for an efficient brainstorming meeting:

- ✓ A quiet location with few distractions.
- ✓ A specific purpose of which participants are aware.
- ✓ An understanding of the meeting's purpose and the eventual goals for the ideas gathered.
- ✓ A talented facilitator that can lead attendees in productive discussion.
- ✓ Ground rules for participating in the meeting to ensure all voices are heard.

**Here are some expressions that are useful when participating in brainstorming meetings.**

### Changing topics
- By the way...
- That reminds me...
- Speaking about..., I heard that...
- Before I forget...
- It just occurred to me that...
- This isn't related to what we're talking about, but...
- Sorry to change the subject for a minute...

### Adding information
- I'd like to add something...
- Furthermore,
- To continue, I think that...
- Like you were saying,

### Refusing an offer
- I'm sorry, but I'm going to have to decline.
- Thank you for the offer, but that is not necessary.
- It's really kind of you to ask, but I have to turn you down.
- Unfortunately, I'm going to have to say no.
- I'm afraid that's not possible.

## Let's Practice
- » Sharing independent research
- » Suggesting an alternative plan
- » Disagreeing with a co-worker

# Simulation.7

## Case Study (Group)

### A. Background

Buzz Cola is a new energy drink and cola combination that has taken the European market by storm. The German beverage manufacturers feel that the product is an excellent fit for the Indian market, and they hope to begin distributing it with their other international products as soon as they can come up with a good marketing strategy. A huge part of the brand's success in other markets has been sponsorship efforts, with Buzz Cola spending large sums of money on brand placement on television and at popular sporting events.

### B. Task

The company is in the initial phases of developing this strategy. They are hosting a brainstorming meeting with a team from the company's local Indian distributor as well as the corporate marketing strategy team.

**They want to generate ideas regarding :**
- Events for sponsorship
- A region-appropriate slogan for the project
- Packaging

### C. Roles

**FORMAL vs. INFORMAL** — How would a formal meeting be different to an informal meeting in this senario?

#### Participant A : Indian Distributer Representative

- ✓ Suggests product placements in Hollywood movies and ads during popular sporting events, such as cricket.
- ✓ Thinks promoting the product's European image has an advantage.
- ✓ Has a marketing team testing the product's current European slogan in test groups with successful results.
- ✓ Wants to use international celebrity sponsors.

#### Participant B : Buzz Cola Marketing Strategy Team Member

- ✓ Wants to find suggestions for television opportunities.
- ✓ Has limited ideas for ad designs and new slogans.
- ✓ Wants to keep the brand packaging consistent worldwide.

## ✳ Meeting preparation

- Was a meeting time and place set in advance? ✓
- Was a clear agenda set? Were participants notified beforehand? ☐
- Were participants chosen for specific skills? ☐

## ✳ Meeting roles and responsibilities

- Is there a designated facilitator? ☐
- Are all participants aware of their role for the meeting? ☐
- Do the hosts act accordingly to their role? ☐
- Do the guests act accordingly to their role? ☐

## ✳ Meeting procedure

- Was someone tasked with recording minutes? ☐
- Was the agenda established at the start of the meeting? ☐
- Was there sufficient time to cover each topic? ☐
- Was time given to evaluate various ideas? ☐

## ✳ Meeting follow-up

- Was the desired outcome achieved? If not, what will the next step be? ☐
- Was a deadline established for any tasks assigned? ☐
- Is a follow-up meeting necessary? ☐
- Was there anything that could be improved on before the next meeting? ☐

## ✳ Effective meeting language

- Did participants stay on topic? ☐
- Did interruptions occur only when necessary? ☐
- Was positive participation encouraged? ☐
- Were all attendees asked to provide input? ☐

## ✳ Brainstorming meeting tactics

- Was free expression encouraged? ☐
- Do any ideas introduced need further research? ☐
- Has a plan been made for the next meeting? ☐
- Were roles assigned in the action plans? ☐

---

### Tips!

- India has a group-oriented culture. As a result, championing personal views might be considered less important than being a part of a group and fitting in well with its members.

- Indians tend to respect hierarchy. If an Indian views you as a superior, he or she may be reluctant to give you honest feedback on your ideas. Instead, he or she may simply try to tell you what you seem to want to hear.

## " Effective Brainstorming Checklist "

**Chapter. 8**

# Setting and Environment

## Have you ever...

Have you ever forgotten an important detail when planning a meeting? There are many tasks that need to be completed for a well-organized meeting. When finishing up last-minute preparations, it can be easy to overlook something. While individual details may seem unimportant, even the small things contribute to the overall feel of a meeting. In situations where something goes wrong, it takes quick thinking to get everything to run smoothly.

**Look at the statements below and discuss how you would act in each situation.**

1. Five minutes before the start of the meeting, you discover that the computer in the meeting room does not have the software program you need for your presentation.

2. You realize too late that there are not enough chairs for the meeting guests.

3. The conference room is occupied by another team that did not formally reserve it.

4. You need to call a last-minute meeting, but all the meeting rooms are reserved.

5. The air conditioner is broken in the room you have reserved, and the hot room is making attendees drowsy.

# A gentleman says
**Look at the expressions. How do they differ?**

| GENERAL LANGUAGE | GENTLEMAN |
|---|---|
| 1. Want something to drink? | → *Would you like something to drink?* |
| 2. Let's sit down. | → *Could everyone please take their seats?* |
| 3. Can everyone see okay? | → *Does anyone need to move to see?* |
| 4. Take a handout and pass them down. | → *Would you please pass down the handouts?* |
| 5. Is the temperature good for everyone? | → *Would anyone like me to adjust the thermostat?* |

## Meeting Room Layout

### Exercise 1

Setting up a meeting room includes prepping the area where the meeting will take place in advance. This involves a wide range of tasks including physically bringing in all relevant materials, such as :

|1| Having the correct number of printouts or handouts
|2| Setting up special equipment such as a speaker system, smart board, or projector
|3| Preparing beverages and other snacks
|4| Arranging and laying out the correct number of chairs and desks

**Effective Meeting Skills**

**HOW TO...** (ANS)

You are responsible for arranging a conference room for an upcoming meeting. Read through the details below and decide what type of seating arrangement would best fulfill your group's needs. Draw a quick diagram of how you would arrange the room.

✓ Group of 12.
✓ Two presenters will need to use a computer and a projector.
✓ The screen is located on the front wall.
✓ The arrangement should allow for group discussion.
✓ Refreshments and light snacks will be served.

**HINTS! TYPICAL ROOM SET UP REQUESTS**

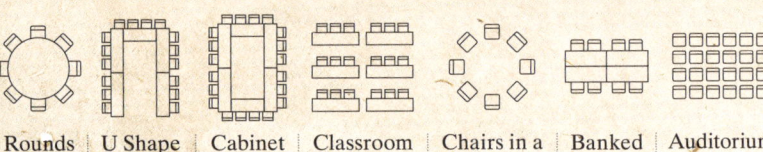

Rounds | U Shape Cabinet | Cabinet | Classroom | Chairs in a Circle | Banked Cabinet | Auditorium

# Break Time Conversation

**Exercise 2**

Break time conversations help create a pleasant meeting atmosphere as well as build strong working relationships. By using small talk effectively, you can learn a little more about your colleagues and help further your professional and private agendas.

> When making small talk, it is important to avoid controversial topics, such as politics and religion. People love to talk about themselves, so it is just as important to be a good listener as it is to be a good storyteller. Try to ask open-ended questions that give the other person an opportunity to tell about him or herself.

## HOW TO... ANS

**Partner work**

Work in pairs. You and a partner are discussing whether the topics are suitable (O) or inappropriate (X) for small talk. Then practice good break time conversation.

- ____ Vacation plans
- ____ A mutual acquaintance
- ____ Recent weather
- ____ A sports championship
- ____ A mistake a presenter made
- ____ Local election results
- ____ Company layoffs
- ____ An upcoming long weekend
- ____ An interesting picture on the wall
- ____ Children's accomplishments

memo.

# Meeting DIY
## Setting and Environment

Review the skills and ideas you have learned in this chapter that will help you to effectively organize meeting settings and environments. Use the space provided below to create a personal action plan and set goals for meetings in the future.

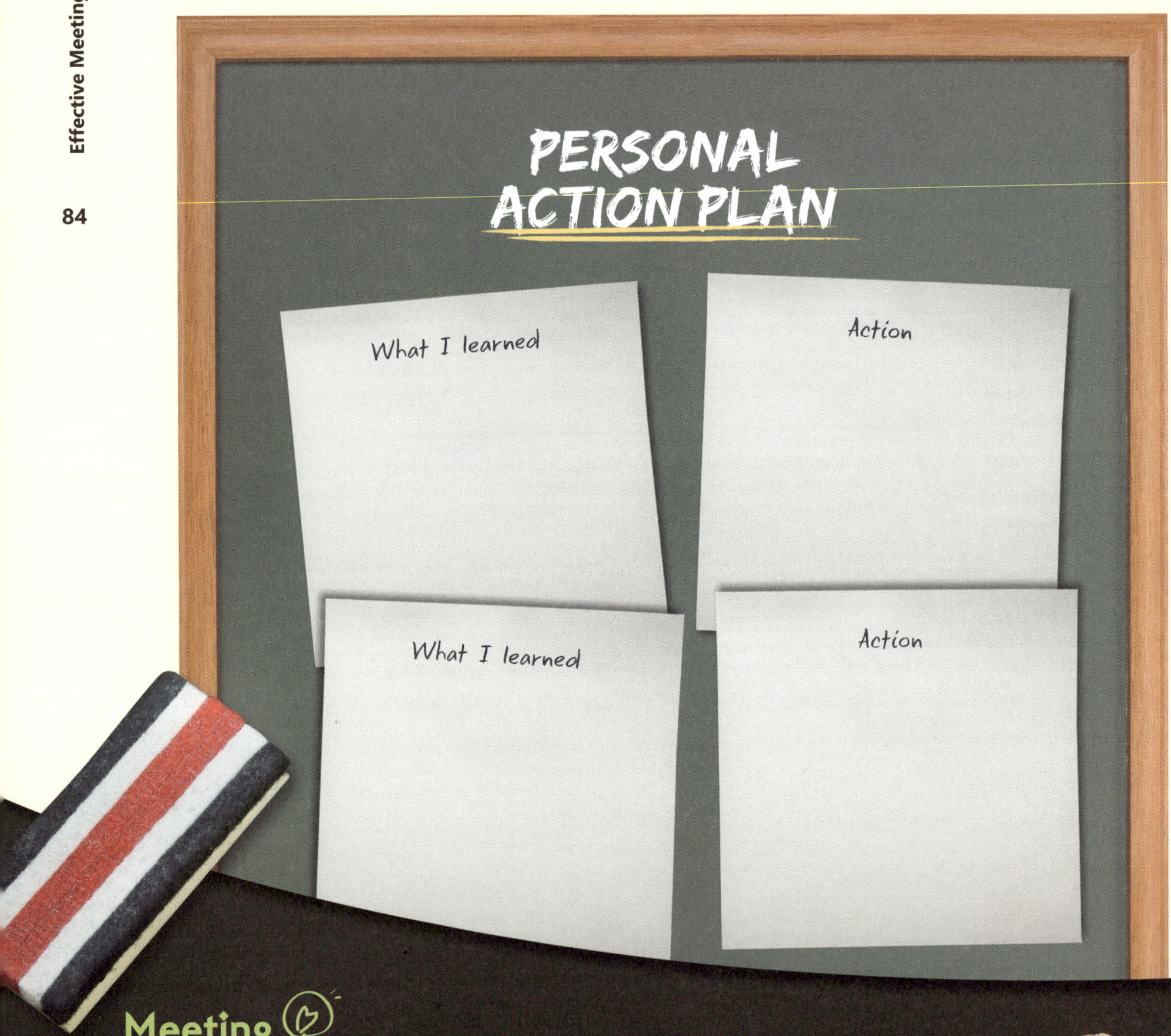

## PERSONAL ACTION PLAN

- What I learned
- Action
- What I learned
- Action

## Meeting Skills TIP

**It's all about the layout.** – Positioning of seating and tables is important, and for certain types of meetings it's crucial. Ensure the layout is appropriate for the occasion. Also, make sure that all participants have a clear view of any screens, charts, or visual materials.

# Simulation 08

## Decision-making meetings

are internal meetings where the desired result is an agreement regarding a specific issue. In these meetings, participants might listen to multiple sides of an argument and then be asked to deliberate until all parties come to a consensus.

**In order to run an efficient decision-making meeting, it is important to :**
- ✓ Be aware of individual attendees' interests and agendas.
- ✓ Appoint a neutral facilitator who will be able to guide the discussion without being influenced by office politics.
- ✓ Formulate thoughts regarding the matter in advance.
- ✓ Attempt to understand the pros and cons of both sides of the argument.

**Here are some expressions that are useful when participating in decision-making meetings.**

### Expressing a lack of understanding
- I beg your pardon?
- I'm not quite sure what you mean.
- I'm sorry, but I don't follow.
- I don't quite see what you're getting at.
- I'm not sure I get your point.

### Disputing a claim
- I'm afraid that I don't agree with you on that.
- I agree up to a point, but…
- That's not how I see it.
- If you consider the evidence…
- That may be true, but…
- It's unjustifiable to say that…

### Keeping a conversation going
- What happened after…?
- How did that make you feel?
- How did you react?
- That's so interesting. What did you do next?

### Let's Practice
» Making small talk before a meeting
» Trying to persuade someone over to your side
» Offering an alternative course of action

# Simulation 8

## Case Study (Group)

### A Background

AXA is a rapidly growing fashion retailer headed by the Moroccan fashion designer Tewfik Allal. The company is headquartered in Marrakech and currently operates more than 200 locations in northern Africa and continental Europe. AXA designs, produces, and markets their unique designs in company-owned retail locations. Currently, AXA is looking for opportunities to test the North American market without committing to investing in freestanding stores.

### B Task

The marketing team must decide which approach to recommend for launching their brand in the U.S. Team members have been researching the pros and cons of various short-term distribution models. During the past few weeks, they have discussed the issue at length, and the group is finally nearing the end of the decision-making process. Today, three team members will review the key points of their research before coming to an agreement.

### C Roles

**FORMAL vs. INFORMAL** — How would a formal meeting be different to an informal meeting in this senario?

**Participant A: Marketing Team Member 1**
- ✓ In favor of opening temporary pop-up shops in major cities.
- ✓ Would require higher overhead costs.
- ✓ Would let the company operate within their comfort zone and test their current products on the American market without a long-term commitment.

**Participant B: Marketing Team Member 2**
- ✓ Wants to launch a collaborative collection with a nationwide discount retail chain.
- ✓ Would give them wider distribution with an established network of stores.
- ✓ Would require a two-year contract during which they would be prohibited from opening their own retain locations.
- ✓ Might involve sacrificing quality to lower production costs.

**Participant C: Marketing Team Member 3**
- ✓ Wants to place their current line in mid-range regional department store chain.
- ✓ Would allow them to maintain the same product quality.
- ✓ Could test their products on a regional market.
- ✓ Would be free to open retail locations at a time of their choosing while maintaining their relationship with the chain.

## *Meeting preparation

- Was a meeting time and place set in advance? ✓
- Was a clear agenda set? Were participants notified in advance? ☐
- Were participants chosen for specific skills? ☐
- Did the attendees have special responsibilities? ☐

## *Meeting setting and environment

- Was the meeting location set up according to the meeting style? ☐
- Was the meeting room set up with the required equipment? ☐
- Was the meeting room layout suitable to the meeting proceedings? ☐
- Was the meeting atmosphere well managed? ☐

## *Meeting procedure

- Was someone tasked with recording minutes? ☐
- Was the agenda set at the start of the meeting? ☐
- Was sufficient time scheduled to cover each topic? ☐
- Was time given to evaluate various ideas? ☐

## *Meeting follow-up

- Was the desired outcome achieved? If not, what will the next step be? ☐
- Was a deadline established for any tasks assigned? ☐
- Is a follow-up meeting necessary? ☐
- Was there anything that could be improved on before the next meeting? ☐

## *Effective meeting language

- Did participants stay on topic? ☐
- Did interruptions occur only when necessary? ☐
- Was positive participation encouraged? ☐
- Were all participants asked to provide input? ☐

## *Decision-making meeting tactics

- Were the pros and cons of the decision fully explored? ☐
- Does any aspect need further research? ☐
- Has a plan been made for the next meeting? ☐
- Were roles assigned in the action plans? ☐

---

**Tips!**

- In some cultures, decision-making is a slow process. Moroccans rarely view an offer as final. Avoid rushing them to make a decision or your actions could be perceived as insulting.

- Relationship-building is important in Morocco. Be prepared to spend time building trust. Moroccans would prefer wasting time and money to hastily jumping into an agreement with a partner that they are not sure about.

---

"Effective Decision-making Checklist"

# Chapter. 9

## Writing Technique

### Have you ever...

Have you ever been asked to take minutes in an important meeting? Providing an accurate and organized record is a huge responsibility. Simultaneously listening, summarizing, and recording events is a challenging task that can give even the most experienced office workers a little stress. What happens when you fall behind?

**WHAT SHOULD YOU DO?**

*Group*

**Read the following situations. With a partner prepared how you would react and handle each situation.**

**Situation A**
You can't find the standard template for writing minutes.

**Situation B**
You are involved in a topic that is being discussed and are having trouble balancing taking minutes and talking.

**Situation C**
Everyone is speaking at once and you are having trouble keeping up with your notes.

**Situation D**
The conversation has become very long and confusing and you aren't sure what parts should be written down.

**Situation E**
The discussion is jumping from topic to topic without any clear conclusions to record.

# A gentleman says
**Look at the expressions. How do they differ?**

### GENERAL LANGUAGE
1. Take the minutes, Sam.
2. Help me with this handout.
3. Could you read over this for me?
4. This sounds right.
5. Is anyone missing?
6. Did I get everything?

### GENTLEMAN
→ *Would you mind taking the minutes, Sam?*
→ *Could you please help me prepare the handout?*
→ *I would like your help proofreading this.*
→ *Everything seems to be in order.*
→ *Is everyone in attendance?*
→ *Does anyone else have something to add?*

# Presentation and Handout Materials

**Exercise 1**

Meeting handouts create a lasting impression of your presentation. They play a valuable role in demonstrations as they help the speaker avoid overwhelming an audience with information. By providing everything in writing, handouts ensure that no important details are completely forgotten. They also aid listeners by making sure that they leave with all the necessary facts.

### Writing effective presentation handouts

1. Prepare in advance to avoid sloppy looking printouts.
2. Make sure your handout adds value to your key messages.
3. Strive to supply each member of your audience with a handout that provides follow-up contact details.
4. Make your handout look impressive, professional and authoritative.
5. Provide blank spaces for note-taking.
6. Presentation handout must be relevant to your audience.
7. Formulate the layout to be appealing and concise.

## HOW TO...

What makes a good handout? Use the area provided to brainstorm of the essential characteristics that make a good handout. Finish up by writing a list of all the things that must be included in a meeting handout.

# Meeting Minutes

### Exercise 2

Meeting minutes are a written record of the major details of a meeting beginning with a list of attendees. Then the note-taker should record the issues covered during the course of the meeting, as well as decisions made. When writing minutes, it is important to focus on summarizing the basics of what was discussed and record what was decided or assigned. The minute scan be used to formally designate tasks and set action plans, so accurate record-keeping is a must.

**When writing minutes :**
- Focus on decisions and action plans, not conversations themselves.
- Use the same tense throughout and avoid using names unless recording a motion or second.
- Refrain from writing personal observations and stay as neutral as possible. The less descriptive your writing is, the better.

Minutes are meant to provide an outline of what occurred during a meeting, not an exact transcript of what was said. Paraphrase the following statements to fit into a meeting outline.

| | |
|---|---|
| Janet | We need to go into this topic in more depth. I make a motion to assign a team to research the cost of breaking ground on the Linden Avenue project. |
| Deborah | I second the motion. |
| Chair | All in favor? All opposed? Let the record show that the motion passed 9 to 1. |

**Paraphrase**

---

| | |
|---|---|
| Chair | Alex Reed will take over the Clayton account when Mr. Williams retires. If there are no further points to be discussed, the meeting is adjourned. |

**Paraphrase**

---

| | |
|---|---|
| Ben | I motion to postpone this topic until the next meeting of the board. |
| Samuel | I second the motion. |
| Chair | All in favor? The conversation has been tabled to next week's agenda. |

**Paraphrase**

---

| | |
|---|---|
| Chair | Let's get started. First off, I want to thank you all for coming, and I would like to extend a special welcome to Theodore Grey, who is visiting us from Brightwood Industries. Before we move on to new business, I'd like to briefly go over our agenda for today. |

**Paraphrase**

# Meeting DIY
## Writing Technique

Review the skills and ideas you have learned in this chapter that will help you to effectively prepare written meeting documents. Use the space provided below to create a personal action plan and set goals for meetings in the future.

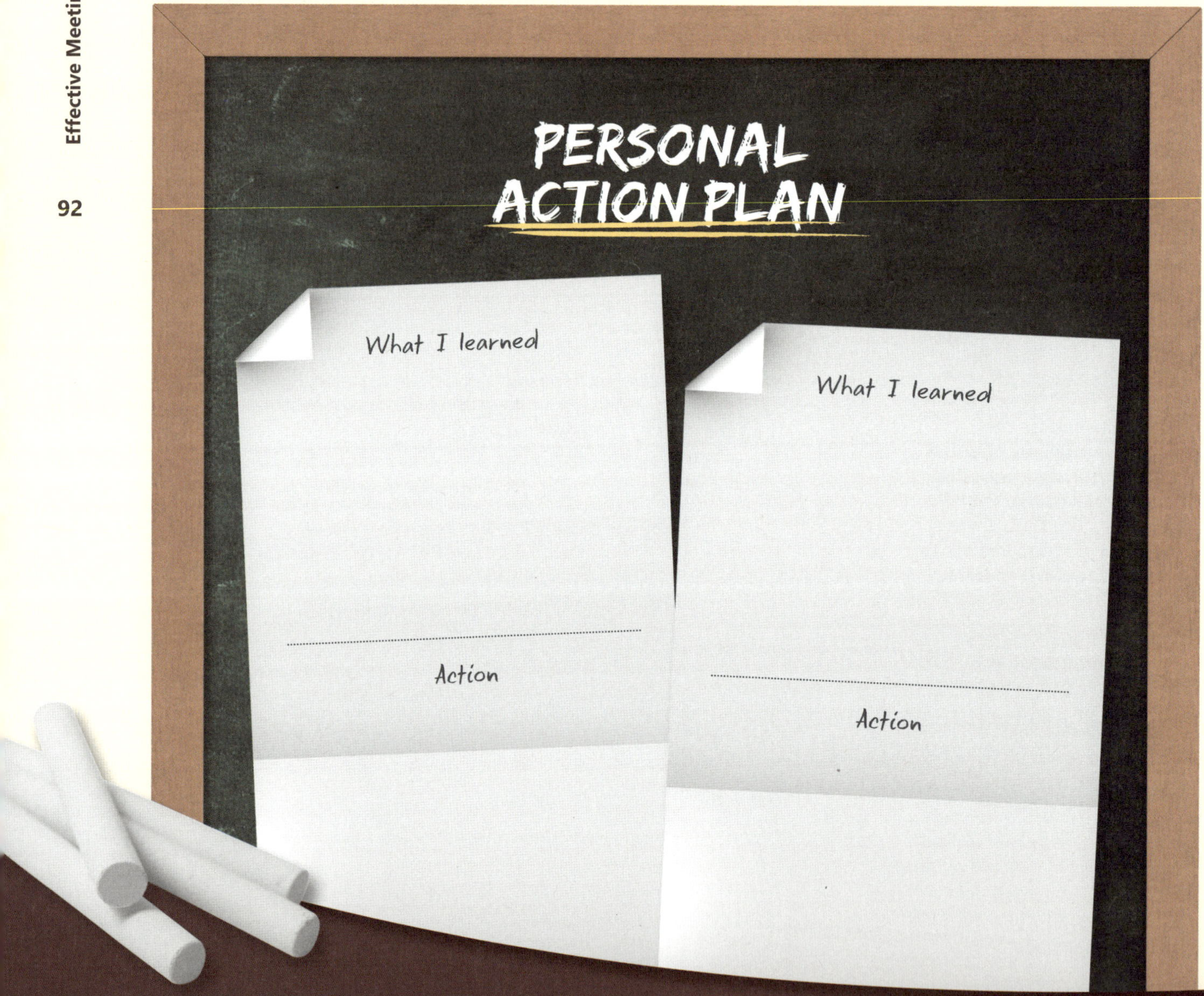

## PERSONAL ACTION PLAN

**What I learned**

_____

**Action**

**What I learned**

_____

**Action**

## Meeting Skills TIP

**Clarification is key.** – In meetings judgments are often made before all participants know what they are discussion. It is important that all members understand what they are discussing, and the impacts of their discussions. Clarify the topic of debate and any ideas or suggestions that others make if anything is unclear before making a decision.

# Simulation 09

## A consultation meeting

is a kind of internal meeting that involves bringing in experts from other departments or outside of the company to advise on a specific issue or fill a need in a short-term project. There are many reasons a company may seek to do this, including lack of expertise, being stuck in the development stage, or insufficient staffing. Bringing in an outside consultant can offer access to assets that are not necessary in their ordinary scope of work.

### The benefits of consultants include :

- ✓ Gaining skills that current employees lack.
- ✓ Hearing an objective outsider's viewpoint.
- ✓ Receiving honest feedback from someone who isn't worried about upsetting co-workers.
- ✓ Profiting from a temporary boost in resources.

**Good to Know**

Here are some expressions that are useful when involved in a consultation.

### Giving good news

- We are pleased to announce…
- It has been a record-breaking year for…
- The…has been a resounding success.
- … have far exceeded our expectations.

### Offering sympathy

- … must be really difficult for you.
- You are handling…really well.
- I understand how…that must be.
- I really respect the way you…
- The situation couldn't be avoided.

### Inspiring hope

- We are confident that…
- I hope this will reassure you of…
- The situation will be rectified…
- We hope to regain…

**Let's Practice**

» Explaining a poor economic situation
» Apologizing for a careless error
» Announcing expansion plans

# Simulation 9

## Case Study (Group) — Effective Meeting Skills

### A) Background

Navisoft is a small Australian software company that designs, installs and maintains network security systems for financial institutions. They are well established in the banking industry and have an excellent reputation for both product quality and customer service. Recently one of their key security programs was hacked, and this has resulted in a great deal of negative publicity for the firm. Due to the high media coverage of the problem, the in-house PR team feels ill-equipped to cope with the issue internally and would like to consult with someone more experienced with this type of situation.

### B) Task

The Navisoft in-house PR team will consult with Harrison PR Solutions, a large PR firm that specializes in damage control. They will discuss the best way to minimize the situation and handle the issue before lasting damage to the company's image has been caused. Due to the sensitive nature of the security industry, Navisoft is reluctant to reveal too much about the situation and the measures that they used to repair the system to the public.

### C) Roles

**FORMAL vs. INFORMAL** — How would a formal meeting be different to an informal meeting in this senario?

**Participant A : Navisoft PR Team Member**
- ✓ Is open to suggestions about what approach to take.
- ✓ Wants to reassure the public that the situation has been resolved.
- ✓ Feels consumer confidence is critical to their brand.
- ✓ Cannot give industry information about the new security protocols to the outside consultant.

**Participant B : Harrison PR Solutions Consultant**
- ✓ Feels an honest public statement from the Navisoft CEO is the best approach.
- ✓ Needs some details about the new security protocols to reassure clients.
- ✓ Wants to emphasize the prompt way that the company dealt with the situation.

# "Effective Consultations Checklist"

> **Tips!**
> - The main difference between a consultant and a surrogate manager is that a consultant is unable to makes decisions for their employer, while a surrogate manager has decision-making authority.
> - When choosing whether or not to hire a consultant, it is important to consider whether or not the company has the internal capability to deal with the problem on their own and whether or not there are any benefits to hiring an outside consultant.

## ✲ Meeting preparation
- Was a meeting time and place set? ✓
- Have attendees been invited? ☐
- Has the fee for the consultant been set? ☐
- Are there any special documents or access codes that the consultant will need? ☐

## ✲ Writing techniques
- Were handouts prepared beforehand? ☐
- Were presentation and consultation materials organized before the meeting? ☐
- Was a template provided for the meeting minutes? ☐

## ✲ Meeting follow-up
- Was there any unfinished business? If so, is there a plan to address it? ☐
- Will there be an additional meeting? ☐
- Do all relevant people have the consultant's contact information? ☐
- How long will the professional relationship continue? ☐

## ✲ Effective meeting language
- Were all contributions polite? ☐
- Was time spent evaluating ideas and finding solutions? ☐
- Were the results of the consultant's work clearly presented? ☐
- Was time given for feedback and questions? ☐

## ✲ Meeting procedure
- Was the consultant introduced to other participants? ☐
- Was a moderator for the meeting appointed? ☐
- Was the purpose of the meeting clarified? ☐
- Did participants stick to the agenda? ☐
- Were the consultant's knowledge and outside resources sufficiently utilized? ☐

## ✲ Consultation meeting tactics
- Were all internal attendees receptive to what the consultant had to say? ☐
- Was the consultant given access to necessary materials? ☐
- Was an action plan made to utilize the consultant's expertise? ☐
- Was the consultant given sufficient time to speak? ☐

**Chapter. 10**

# Meeting Etiquette

## Have you ever...

Have you ever been offended by someone during the course of a meeting? Maybe someone forgot to give you credit or a coworker interrupted your presentation to offer a bit of not-so-constructive criticism. When business etiquette is ignored, it can negatively affect employee performance and the overall productivity of a meeting. To make sure your meeting is a success, try to keep conversation polite and on topic.

Read the following situations. With a partner prepared how you would react and handle each situation.

- Situation A

Someone tells an inappropriate joke, and you feel upset.

- Situation B

Someone keeps interrupting you.

- Situation C

You were stuck in traffic and missed the beginning of the meeting.

- Situation D

Someone brought a cell phone, and it keeps vibrating on the table.

- Situation E

Someone showed up to the meeting obviously unprepared (no pencil, no documents, etc.).

# A gentleman says
Look at the expressions. How do they differ?

### GENERAL LANGUAGE

1. Just let me finish.
2. Don't interrupt, Martha.
3. That doesn't seem accurate.
4. Calm down. I think you misunderstood me.
5. You're looking at this too superficially.
6. Like Bill was saying, we need to increase our advertising budget.

### GENTLEMAN

→ *Could you please wait until after I'm finished?*
→ *Just a moment, Martha. I'll come back to you when Pete is finished.*
→ *I'd be interested in reading your research on the subject.*
→ *I'm sorry, but I think there was a misunderstanding.*
→ *I think this issue needs further consideration.*
→ *As Bill suggested, increasing our advertising budget is necessary.*

## Making apologies

### Exercise 1

Apologies involve acknowledging an offense or failure to make someone feel better. When done carefully, an apology can help further agendas. When done hastily or halfheartedly, an apology can make a tense situation even worse. There are several things that are important to consider when preparing to apologize that ensures that your message is accepted.

**When making an apology, it is important to:**

1. Choose how to deliver your apology: face-to-face or in writing.
2. Decide on the best time to make an apology; an immediate apology is usually best.
3. Express regret in a sincere manner.
4. Avoid making excuses or blaming others.
5. Try to see things from the other person's point of view when deciding what to say.
6. Admit what you did wrong.

## HOW TO...

Read through the following situations. What kind of apology is necessary? Act out each situation with a partner.

### Situation A

Your cell phone battery died during the night, so your alarm didn't go off. As a result, you slept through an important client meeting, and your team member was forced to improvise through your part of the presentation. When you woke up and realized what happened, you discovered more than 10 missed calls from various team members.

### Situation B

You have been overloaded with work lately and barely made your deadline for a quarterly progress report. You had to rush through it and were unable to proofread it thoroughly. After presenting the report at a meeting, you realized that there were many typos and other errors in the report.

### Situation C

You promised a client that their order would be delivered by next Monday, but you forgot to check the inventory first. You have since discovered that the product is backordered and that it will take at least two weeks for the shipment to be prepared.

# Interruptions

**Exercise 2**

An interruption is an act or utterance that temporarily disrupts someone else. In business meetings, this is sometimes necessary to get clarification on a point or to have your opinion heard. When done correctly, a short interruption will not disrupt the flow of a meeting; however, brusque interruptions can throw a meeting off-course and cause hurt feelings.

**Interruptions :**
- Should be relevant to what is being discussed.
- Somehow improve or clarify the conversation.
- Should begin by expressing some regret about interrupting the speaker.
- Are more effective when they include a summary of what was said by the speaker to explain why what you want to say is relevant.
- Should be short and to-the-point.

**Match the phrases with similar meanings. How could these phrases be used when interrupting?**

1. You have an excellent point.
2. May I interrupt?
3. One person at a time, please.
4. I'd like to add something.
5. Please let me finish what I was saying.
6. I just want to point out that this is only a temporary solution.
7. Could you please wait until after the presentations are finished?

a. Not everyone can speak at once.
b. Could I finish first?
c. I agree with what you are saying.
d. I'd like to remind you that this is only a temporary fix.
e. May I interject?
f. Could you hold questions until after the presentations are finished?
g. I have something I'd like to say.

# Meeting DIY

## Meeting Etiquette

Review the skills and ideas you have learned in this chapter that will help you to keep to global business meeting etiquette. Use the space provided below to create a personal action plan and set goals for meetings in the future.

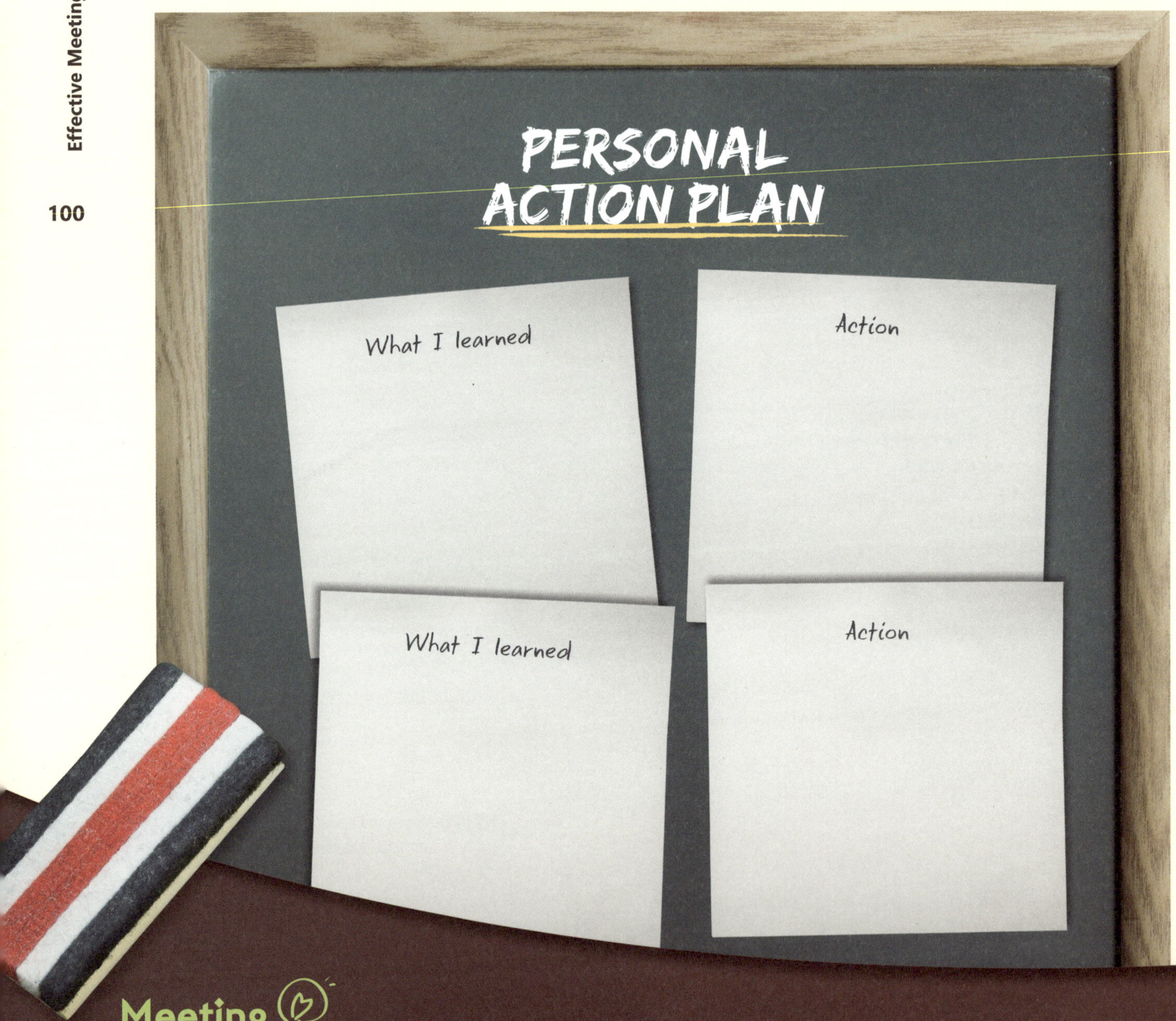

## PERSONAL ACTION PLAN

| What I learned | Action |
| --- | --- |
| What I learned | Action |

### Meeting Skills TIP

**Conflict is necessary and helpful.** – While being polite and having good business etiquette is key to becoming a respected and successful business person, in meetings a certain amount of conflict is necessary and helpful. Effective meetings will bring a conflict into the open and deal with it transparently. Make sure that conflicts are resolved rather than pushed aside or out of the way.

# Simulation 10

## Negotiation meetings

are typically where the details of a deal between multiple parties are fine-tuned. Most negotiations occur face-to-face. As a result, giving off an organized first impression is critical. Proper planning and skillful meeting management could make or break a deal. The greater the complexity of a negotiation is, the more important the planning and execution of the meeting becomes.

**Negotiation meeting factors to plan :**

- ✓ **Attendance :** Who should attend, how long each person must be present for, whether team or individual attendance should be required, attendees' roles and responsibilities
- ✓ **Agenda :** Who is responsible for its writing, what issues should appear, how issues should be ordered
- ✓ **Venue :** Formal or informal, your office or your partner's
- ✓ **Length of the meeting :** Including any necessary breaks
- ✓ **Style of negotiation favored :** Collaborative or competitive
- ✓ **Staging of meetings :** Relationship-building may be the initial priority with details to follow in a later meeting
- ✓ **Concession strategy :** How to make effective compromises and not sacrifice too much

### Good to Know

Here are some expressions that are useful when in a negotiation.

### Defending positions
- Let me put it another way...
- I think the point I'm trying to make here is...
- Well, if you could just spare me a moment...
- Understanding the idea requires deliberation.
- The crux of the issue is...

### Asking for more time
- Let's think about it.
- How about giving it a little more thought?
- Could you give me more time to think about it?
- I'm not sure we should rush into anything today.
- Could I get back to you on that?

### Expressing partial agreement
- I agree with you to some extent, but...
- Your point of view is fine, but...
- I think you are on the right track, but...
- That may be true, but...

**Let's Practice**
» Talking about budgets
» Talking about deadlines
» Handling problems

# Simulation.10

## Case Study (Group)

### A. Background

Green Solutions (GS) is a U.S.-based multinational company that specializes in renewable energy and solar power. In China, the company has successfully established joint ventures with several medium-sized municipalities to provide green solutions for public companies that are looking to lower their energy consumption and reduce waste. To increase its holdings in China, GS has arranged to enter into a strategic alliance with Xiang and Co., a Chinese conglomerate with strong roots in China's manufacturing industry. The venture is called Haoyuan China Limited (HCL).

### B. Task

The representatives of HCL have been negotiating with a large-sized municipal organization for a contract to develop a solar power station. HCL has submitted a proposal for the contract with some details to be negotiated with the municipal's board members.

> **The unresolved issues are :**
> - Duration of the project (Negotiable: 15-16months)
> - Ratio of domestic and foreign investment capital (7:3)
> - Organization structure of the project (shareholders, etc.)

### C. Roles

 **FORMAL vs. INFORMAL** — How would a formal meeting be different to an informal meeting in this scenario?

**Participant A : HCL representative**

- ✓ Wants the project duration to be 16 months.
- ✓ Organization structure does not matter greatly so long as a direct line of contact is established between the two parties.
- ✓ Aims to have the ratio of foreign to domestic investments to be 6:4 respectively.

**Participant B : Municipal representative**

- ✓ Wants the project duration to be 14 months.
- ✓ Aims to have the ratio of foreign to domestic investments be 3:7 respectively, but is flexible depending on the duration of the project.
- ✓ Organization structure is extremely important to them.

*Effective Meeting Skills*

# Effective Negotiations Checklist

## ★ Meeting preparation
- Was a meeting time and place set? ✓
- Have attendees been formally invited? ☐
- Did everyone RSVP or notify the organizers that they will be unable to attend? ☐
- Has everyone been told in advance of any special responsibilities that they have? ☐
- Have all necessary documents and equipment been prepared? ☐

## ★ Meeting procedure
- Were all visiting parties properly introduced? ☐
- Was there an icebreaker or a warm-up activity? ☐
- Was someone tasked with recording minutes? ☐
- Was the purpose of the meeting clarified? ☐
- Did participants stick to the agenda? ☐

## ★ Meeting etiquette
- Did all participants follow meeting protocols? ☐
- Were all necessary apologies made? ☐
- Were the interruptions made during the meeting relevant to the subject? ☐
- Were interruptions dealt with correctly? ☐

## ★ Meeting follow-up
- Was there any unfinished business? If so, is there a plan to address it? ☐
- Has a plan been made for the next meeting? ☐
- Will the minutes be distributed? If so, to whom? ☐
- Do any files from the meeting need to be shared? ☐

## ★ Effective meeting language
- Were all parties' views heard? ☐
- Were conflicts dealt with appropriately? ☐
- Was time spent evaluating options and finding compromises? ☐
- Did participants interact positively with one another? ☐

## ★ Negotiation meeting tactics
- Were all necessary documents shared in advance? ☐
- Did you focus on finding common ground with the other group? ☐
- Were all parties on your side aware of what was negotiable? ☐
- Was an agreement reached? If not, what is the next step? ☐

### Tips!
- Did you know that Chinese negotiations are usually attended by all parties involved and followed by a social gathering?
- ZOPA often referred to as the "contracting zone," stands for "Zone of Possible Agreement." It is the range or area in which an agreement is satisfactory to both parties involved in the negotiation process.

# Chapter. 11

## Cross-Cultural Skills

### Have you ever...

Have you ever collaborated on a project with someone from a different cultural background? If so, you may have encountered some perplexing behavior from the other person. Due to cultural differences and the miscommunications that can arise when using a second language, it can be difficult to tell what a person's true intentions are. What is considered impolite in your culture might be encouraged in another. For this reason, it is necessary to approach interactions with people from different cultures with an open mind and a patient attitude.

Read the following situations. With a partner prepared how you would react and handle each situation.

**Situation A**
A visiting business partner is speaking to you in an extremely brusque way and you can't tell if he is angry or if his point is lost in translation.

**Situation B**
A new foreign associate has presented you with an expensive gift and you aren't sure how to react or reciprocate.

**Situation C**
You have been repeatedly interrupted during a presentation by a foreign consultant.

**Situation D**
A group of Arab business partners showed up almost 30 minutes late without apology.

**Situation E**
Your company ordered a catered course lunch featuring barbequed meat for visiting Indian associates, only to discover too late that several are vegetarians.

## A gentleman says
Look at the expressions. How do they differ?

| GENERAL LANGUAGE | GENTLEMAN |
|---|---|
| 1. You're a little late, aren't you? | → Thank you for coming. Traffic is bad this time of day, isn't it? |
| 2. Is there anything I should know about your country's meeting culture? | → Do you have any advice for me about your country's meeting culture? |
| 3. Whoops. I shouldn't have said that. | → I apologize if I was too direct. |
| 4. Why do you keep avoiding eye contact with me? | → Does eye contact make you uncomfortable? |
| 5. South Americans never come on time. | → South Americans have a tendency to arrive late. |
| 6. British people are too serious in meetings. | → The British value professionalism. |

## Punctuality across cultures

**Exercise 1**

### What is it?

Punctuality is an important aspect of doing business. Showing up on time for meetings demonstrates respect for your associates and your dealings together; however the definition of punctuality may differ from country to country. The concept of time is very much grounded in culture. In some societies, people share an unspoken understanding that the actual deadlines differ from the stated ones. Typically, industrialized countries are much more concerned with adhering to schedules than developing ones, where rapid development has caused things are seen to be more open to change.

Try to match the countries below with their expectations related to time. Is your country included in the list? How do your culture's expectations of time differ?

1. Korea — A. Punctuality is seen to show reliability, and it is assumed that people will arrive on time.

2. Spain — B. Reliability is highly valued and a delay of even a few minutes could be offensive.

3. United States — C. This culture is very schedule-orientated. Meeting participants commonly show up early.

4. Ghana — D. This country holds a more relaxed view of time, and tardiness not only goes unpunished, but it is expected.

5. Brazil — E. Lateness is not considered rude, and appointment times are usually viewed as a general goal, rather than a promise.

6. Germany — F. Showing up 30 minutes to an hour late is not uncommon.

7. Sweden — G. This culture places a high value on punctuality. Be prepared to arrive on time or, even better, a few minutes early.

8. Cambodia — H. Arriving late to work is not a cause for concern. Appointments do not need to be strictly adhered to.

# Dealing with differences

**Exercise 2**

Cultural differences have a strong effect on global business. Every country has a unique business culture. By researching the culture that you will be working in, you can avoid misunderstandings with your business partners.

**Read the list of statements about different cultures.**

**Valuing Time :**
In many South American countries, meeting times are viewed as a guideline rather than a strict appointment; however, in Western European countries, it is important to arrive on time if not a little early.

**Formality :**
Americans will encourage people to refer to them by their first name from the first meeting, but in Eastern cultures like Japan, calling someone by their first name is rare outside of families.

**Hierarchies :**
In East Asian countries, age and seniority play a big role in business interactions while Western countries tend to be more egalitarian.

**Dress Code :**
Appropriate dress varies according to office culture and situations, but some societies tend to be more formal than others.

**Meals :**
Americans are fond of mixing business and pleasure; however in Spain and some other Western European countries, it is inappropriate to mix food and work talk.

**Greetings :**
In business settings, a handshake is a necessity; however the length and strength of grip vary by culture. In Brazil, strong eye contact and a firm grip are appropriate, but in China, eye contact should be avoided, and the handshake should be coupled with a light bow.

**Gestures :**
Hand gestures do not mean the same thing from country to country. For instance, a thumbs-up gesture is a sign of a job well done in many cultures; however in Middle Eastern countries, it has an offensive connotation.

## HOW TO...

Imagine a foreign acquaintance of yours is coming to work for a year in your country. They are not familiar with your country's business culture. Write down a tip for each category to help them make an easy transition. Compare your tips for each category with your partner.

- Valuing Time
- Formality
- Hierarchies
- Dress Code
- Greetings
- Meals
- Gestures

**Look at the photo and discuss these questions :**
- What seems to be happening in this photo?
- Which of these greetings do you feel most comfortable exchanging? Give your reasons.
- If you were in the same situation, how would you react?

# Meeting DIY
## Cross-Cultural Skills

Review the skills and ideas you have learned in this chapter that will help you to understand cross-cultural differences that are present in global meetings. Use the space provided below to create a personal action plan and set goals for meetings in the future.

## PERSONAL ACTION PLAN

| What I learned | Action |
|---|---|
|  |  |

| What I learned | Action |
|---|---|
|  |  |

## Meeting Skills TIP

**Mix it up.** – A major mistake when dealing with meetings with diverse cultures is to suggest that those of similar backgrounds, be seated together. Rather than allowing for greater understanding and fluency in a group, it usually has an opposite effect. Once situated amongst their cultural groups, participants will slip into their cultural patterns. It is vital to mix up your seating and meeting arrangements to allow for greater cross-cultural exchange.

Key Expressions 110
Answer Key 119

# Appendix

# Appendix
# Key Expressions

## ◆ Making arrangements

- I'll be in touch with you about that....
- Would it be better to...?
- Could you get back to me by...?
- Would you mind being responsible for...?

## ◆ Checking information

- Could I just confirm one detail?
- Let me check something. Did you say...?
- Are you sure this is accurate?
- I need to do a final check. Is ... right?

## ◆ Returning a call

- I'm calling to get back to you on....
- I'm returning your call about....
- I got your message about....
- I heard you called about....

## ◆ Checking a word

- Is that ... as in...?
- Could you spell that back to me?
- I'm sorry, but how do you spell that?
- Would you mind spelling that for me?

## ◆ Asking about plans

- What do you intend to do about...?
- Have you given any more thought to...?
- Are you intending on...?
- Have you made a decision about...?

## ◆ Asking for clarification

- I'm sorry, but I didn't catch that....
- Would you mind repeating that for me?
- Could you say that one more time?
- You're saying that...?

## ◆ Offering an explanation

- I think ... can be attributed to....
- It's possible that....
- The facts point to....
- It is more than likely that....
- A likely explanation is that....

## ◆ Summing up

- In conclusion....
- Just to recap....
- I'd like to go over the main points again.
- In summary....
- After reviewing all the evidence....
- To wrap things up, I think....

## ◆ Presenting visuals

- As you can see in the chart....
- Here you can see a comparison of....
- This figure refers to....
- You will note a strong upward trend....
- Let me draw your attention to....

## ◆ Offering advice

- Have you considered...?
- Why don't you try...?
- If I were in your situation, I would....
- You should try to....
- I'd be happy to....

## ◆ Reassuring someone

- I can assure you that....
- I guarantee that we will do all that we can to....
- Despite what you may have heard....
- Rest assured that....
- This situation is under control.

## ⬥ Offering an apology

- Will you forgive me for...?
- I should apologize for....
- I have to take the blame for....
- I'm sorry, but I should have....
- ... was completely my fault.
- I'm sorry, but I think there was a misunderstanding.

## ⬥ Requesting feedback

- What are your thoughts on...?
- Would you mind looking over this for me?
- I'd like to get your opinion on....
- If you have a suggestion, I'd love to hear it.
- I'd be interested in hearing what you think about....

## ⬥ Offering criticism

- I think it would be better if you....
- ... needs additional consideration.
- I can foresee difficulties with....
- I'm not sure ... would work, because....
- I've noticed that....
- I think this issue needs further consideration.
- I'd be interested in reading your research on the subject.

## ⬥ Offering a compliment

- I'm impressed with the way you....
- You handled ... really well.
- I have to compliment you on....
- Your ... is admirable.

## ⬥ Offering new information

- I just want to update you on....
- The latest report indicates....
- It has recently been revealed that....
- To keep you apprised of the situation....
- I just want to bring you up to date on....

## ⬥ Asking for elaboration

- Could you expound on...?
- What else can you tell us about...?
- Could you elaborate on...?
- Is there anything else you can tell us?
- Could you tell me a little more about...?
- Could you go into more detail?

## ⬥ Changing topics

- By the way....
- That reminds me....
- Speaking about..., I heard that....
- Before I forget....
- It just occurred to me that....
- This isn't related to what we're talking about, but....
- Sorry to change the subject for a minute....

## ⬥ Adding information

- I'd like to add something....
- Furthermore....
- To continue, I think that....
- Like you were saying....

## ⬥ Refusing an offer

- I'm sorry, but I'm going to have to decline.
- Thank you for the offer, but that is not necessary.
- It's really kind of you to ask, but I have to turn you down.
- Unfortunately, I'm going to have to say no.
- I'm afraid that's not possible.

## ⬥ Expressing a lack of understanding

- I beg your pardon?
- I'm not quite sure what you mean.
- I'm sorry, but I don't follow.
- I don't quite see what you're getting at.
- I'm not sure I get your point.

## ⬥ Disputing a claim

- I'm afraid that I don't agree with you on that.
- I agree up to a point, but....
- That's not how I see it.
- If you consider the evidence....
- That may be true, but....
- It's unjustifiable to say that....

## ⬥ Keeping a conversation going

- What happened after...?
- How did that make you feel?
- How did you react?
- That's so interesting. What did you do next?

## Giving good news

- We are pleased to announce....
- It has been a record-breaking year for....
- The ... has been a resounding success.
- ... have far exceeded our expectations.

## Offering sympathy

- ... must be really difficult for you.
- You are handling ... really well.
- I understand how ... that must be.
- I really respect the way you....
- The situation couldn't be avoided.

## Inspiring hope

- We are confident that....
- I hope this will reassure you of....
- The situation will be rectified....
- We hope to regain....

## Defending positions

- Let me put it another way....
- I think the point I'm trying to make here is....
- Well, if you could just spare me a moment....
- Understanding the idea requires deliberation.
- The crux of the issue is....

## Asking for more time

- Let's think about it.
- How about giving it a little more thought?
- Could you give me more time to think about it?
- I'm not sure we should rush into anything today.
- Could I get back to you on that?

## Expressing partial agreement

- I agree with you to some extent, but....
- Your point of view is fine, but....
- I think you are on the right track, but....
- That may be true, but....

## Organizing a meeting

- Can you make it on...?
- We're planning on....
- We're going to go over....
- What's your team's schedule like?
- Do you have a ... preference?
- Could you RSVP by...?
- Don't forget to....
- Let me write this down.
- What's going to be on the agenda?
- Who's responsible for...?
- I'll pencil it in for....

## Pre-meeting correspondence

- I am writing in response to....
- I am writing to apologize for....
- I am writing to confirm....
- I am writing to inform you....
- I am writing regarding....

## Scheduling meetings

- We need to push back to another date.
- Could we move forward the time?
- Why do you set a date for the meeting?
- I'm sure there is no need to reschedule.
- It would be better to postpone the meeting until a better date.
- Have you set a time?
- Please don't put it off until the last minute.
- Let me schedule it in for Friday.

## Starting a meeting

- Let's get down to business.
- We'd better start.
- OK, shall we start?
- Right, let's begin.
- Hello, thanks for agreeing to see me.
- Hello, it's good of you to come and see me.
- It's good to see you again.
- Shall we get down to business?
- There are a few questions I'd like to ask.
- I'd like to start by welcoming....
- If I can get your attention....
- Let's get down to business.
- ... called this meeting to....

- Let me begin with....
- Could you remind me what...?
- I'd like to briefly go over....
- Have you all seen a copy of the agenda?
- Would you mind starting now?

## Welcoming and introducing participants

- We're very pleased to welcome....
- It's a pleasure to welcome....
- I'd like to welcome....
- I'd like to start by welcoming....
- Please join me in welcoming....
- I'd like to introduce....
- I don't think you've met....
- May I introduce...?
- I'd like to start by thanking everyone for coming out.
- First, I'd like to welcome our guests.

## Stating the principal objectives

- We're here today to....
- Our aim is to....
- I've called this meeting in order to....
- The purpose of this meeting is to....
- By the end of this meeting, we need....

## Defining roles

- Peter, could you take the lead?
- Jane has kindly agreed to give us a report on...?
- Ann, could you let us have a report on...?
- John, would you mind taking the minutes?
- So, Nina, you're going to write up....
- Basically, I'd like you to....
- David has agreed to look into....
- Bill is going to take us through....
- Would you mind taking notes today?

## Length of meeting

- This should take about two hours.
- The meeting is due to finish at....
- We're short on time, so can I ask you to be brief?
- I'm afraid we've run out of time.
- I'd like to keep each item to ten minutes. Otherwise, we'll never get through.
- We agreed on ten minutes per item.
- I would like to aim for a three o'clock finish.
- I would like to finish by four o'clock.
- That's fifteen minutes on this.
- Well, that seems to be all the time we have today.

## Setting the agenda

- As you'll see from the agenda....
- I suggest we take this item first/next/last.
- There are three items on the agenda.
- Is there any other business?
- Have you all received a copy of the agenda?
- Shall we take the points in this order?
- If you don't mind, I'd like to skip item 2 and move on to item 3.
- I suggest we take item 2 last.
- The topic will come up under item 3.
- Has everyone received a copy of the agenda?

## Keeping the meeting on target

- Please be brief.
- I'm afraid that's outside the scope of this meeting.
- Let's get back on track, why don't we?
- That's not really why we're here today.
- Why don't we return to the main focus of today's meeting?
- We'll have to leave that for another time.
- We're beginning to lose sight of the main point.
- Keep to the point, please.
- I think we'd better leave that for another meeting.
- Are we ready to make a decision?

## Opening an item

- Let's start with....
- Shall we begin with...?
- So, the first item on the agenda is....
- I'd suggest we start with....
- Why don't we start with....
- Pete, would you like to kick off?
- Shall we start with...?
- Susan, would you like to introduce this item?

## Next item

- Let's move on to the next item....
- The next item on the agenda is....
- Now we come to the question of....
- So, if there is nothing else we need to discuss, let's move on to the next item.
- If there are no further developments, I'd like to move on to....

## Sticking to the agenda

- Can we just deal with...?
- Let's just deal with....
- Can we come to that in a moment?
- I think we are digressing. Can we come back to the main question?
- I think we're getting side-tracked. The main question is....
- I'm not sure that is strictly relevant. Can we return to...?
- That is outside the scope of this meeting. Can we stick to the agenda, please?

## Closing an item

- Right, I think that covers the first item.
- I think that takes care of the first item.
- Shall we leave that item?
- I think that's everything on that.
- Can we leave this point now and move on to the next item?

## Meeting discussions

- Right, I think that covers the first item.
- The next item on the agenda is....
- Let me emphasize....
- Have you considered...?
- We're missing the point.
- I'm not sure what you mean by....
- I agree, but....
- I'm 100% behind....
- As I said earlier....
- Can I draw your attention to...?
- Somebody mentioned....

## Meeting communication

- I suggest we take that up at another meeting.
- Could I make a suggestion?
- I'm sorry to interrupt, but....
- That's a very good point.
- We haven't heard from ... yet.
- Let's hear what ... has to say
- I can see what you're getting at....
- I understand your concern....
- What do you think?
- In my opinion we should....
- What you're saying is....

## Taking a break

- How about taking a break now?
- Should we pause for an intermission?
- Would you like something to drink?

## Moving off the point

- This might be a good point to mention....
- It's not on the agenda, but....
- By the way....

## Referring forward

- We'll come to that later.
- That point is coming up in a moment.

## Referring back

- As we said earlier....
- You said....
- You know what you said about....
- Somebody mentioned....

## Moving around

- Shall we skip the next item?
- I suggest we take that up in another meeting.
- Why don't we move on to...?
- If nobody has anything else to add, let's....

## Interrupting

- Excuse me, may I interrupt?
- Just a moment....
- May I have a word?
- Could I just comment on that?
- If I may, I think....
- Excuse me for interrupting, but....
- May I say something here?
- Excuse me, may I interrupt?
- Can I say something here?
- May I interrupt?
- I'd like to add something.
- I just want to point out that this is only a temporary solution.
- I'd like to remind you that this is only a temporary fix.
- May I interject?
- I have something I'd like to say.

## Chairperson - interrupting

- OK, John, if I could just interrupt you there....
- Mary, sorry but I'd like to hear some other views on this.
- OK. Thank you, Bob. You've made your point.

## Chairperson - stopping an interruption

- Just a moment, I'll come back to you when Mary is finished.
- We can't all speak at once. One at a time, please.
- Please, let him finish.
- One person at a time, please.
- Could you please wait until after the presentations are finished?
- Not everyone can speak at once.
- Could you hold questions until after the presentations are finished?

## Participant - stopping an interruption

- If I could just finish....
- May I just finish?
- No, just one minute....
- No, wait a moment....
- I haven't finished what I was saying.
- Just let me finish.
- Please let me finish what I was saying.
- Could I finish first?

## Considering alternatives

- Have you considered...?
- What about...?
- There's another way of looking at this.
- Mary's suggestion is worth considering.

## Probing questions

- What exactly do you mean...?
- I'm not sure I really understand....
- Could you go into more detail about...?

## Reflective questions

- So you're worried about...?
- If I understand you....

## Asking for verification

- You did say next week, didn't you? ('did' is stressed)
- Do you mean that...?
- Is it true that...?

## Asking for opinions

- What do you think, Peter?
- What's your opinion?
- Are you positive that...?
- Do you (really) think that...?
- Cathy, can we get your input?
- How do you feel about...?

## Giving opinions

- I think/feel/believe....
- In my opinion, we should....
- In my view....
- My view is....
- I'm positive that....
- I (really) feel that....
- The way I see things....
- If you ask me, I tend to think that....

## Commenting on opinions

- That's a good idea/an excellent idea.
- That's very interesting.
- I'm sure we'd all agree with that.
- That's a very good point/an important point.

## Clarifying

- Let me spell out....
- Have I made that clear?
- Do you see what I'm getting at?
- Let me put this in another way....
- I'd just like to repeat that....
- What you are saying is that....
- Do you mean to say that....
- So what you want to say is....
- That means....
- So basically all it means is....

## Clarity of ideas

- I don't see what you're getting at.
- I'm not sure what you mean.
- I'm not sure what you're saying.
- It's not clear what you mean.

## Asking for clarification

- Could you just explain/clarify...?
- I'd like you to clarify one thing.
- I don't quite follow you. What exactly do you mean?
- I'm afraid I don't quite understand what you are getting at.
- Could you explain how that is going to work?
- I don't see what you mean. Could we have some more details, please?

## Ensuring that everything is clear

- OK, is that clear?
- Let me just clarify one thing.
- Do you all see what I'm getting at?
- So, I hope everything's clear.
- Obviously....
- Clearly....

## Asking for contributions

- We haven't heard from you yet, Peter.
- What do you think about this proposal?
- Would you like to add anything, Vicky?
- Has anyone else got anything to contribute?
- Are there any more comments?

## Waiting to be convinced

- I can see what you're getting at.
- There are two sides to the argument.
- On the other hand....
- I'm not sure/convinced about....
- I just think we need more time.

## Relevance of ideas

- We're missing the point.
- We're getting off the point.
- Let's get back to the main point.
- She has a good point.

## Problems of time

- We're rather short on time.
- I'm afraid we're running out of time.
- We'll have to leave that to another time.
- We're behind schedule.
- We're running a little short on time now.

## Giving someone the opportunity to speak

- We haven't heard from Peter.
- Can we hear what Sylvia has to say?
- Just let Thomas finish.

## Total disagreement

- I totally disagree.
- I couldn't agree less.

## Limited agreement

- I agree, but....
- I'm not against it, but....
- Yes, I'm with you.

## ❖ Responding positively

- That's marvelous.
- That's great.
- That's fine.

## ❖ Responding neutrally

- OK.
- All right.
- I see your point.
- I understand your concern.

## ❖ Total commitment

- I'm 100% behind you.
- I entirely agree with you.

## ❖ Completing the agenda

- Right, it looks we've covered the main areas/main points.
- I think that just about covers everything.
- Is there any other business?
- Is there anything more to discuss?

## ❖ Summarizing

- Before we close, let me just summarize the main points.
- Shall I just go over the main points?
- So, to sum up....
- I think we should end here. Just to summarize....
- We've covered everything, so I'd like to go over the decisions we've taken....
- So, to conclude ... we've agreed....

## ❖ Confirming action

- We'll contact....
- Jane will....
- We've got to....
- We need to look at....

## ❖ Asking for repetition

- I'm afraid I didn't understand that. Could you repeat what you just said?
- I didn't catch that. Could you repeat that, please?
- I missed that. Could you say it again, please?
- Could you run that by me one more time?

## ❖ Commenting

- That's interesting.
- I've never thought about it that way before.
- Good point!
- I get your point.
- I see what you mean.

## ❖ Requesting information

- Please, could you...?
- I'd like you to....
- Would you mind...?
- I wonder if you could....
- I suggest we go round the table first.
- I'd like to hear what you all think before we make a decision.

## ❖ Agreeing

- I totally agree with you.
- Exactly!
- That's (exactly) the way I feel.
- I have to agree with George.

## ❖ Disagreeing

- Unfortunately, I see it differently.
- Up to a point, I agree with you, but....
- (I'm afraid) I can't agree.

## ❖ Advising and suggesting

- Let's....
- We should....
- Why don't you...?
- How/What about...?
- I suggest/recommend that....

## ❖ Making recommendations

- I strongly recommend....
- There's no alternative but to....
- I propose/suggest/recommend....
- Why don't we...?
- Perhaps we could consider....
- Maybe we should think about....

## ❖ Dealing with recent developments

- Bill, can you tell us how the XYZ project is progressing?
- Dorothy, how is the XYZ project coming along?
- Cathy, have you completed the report on the new accounting package?
- Has everyone received a copy of the Tate Foundation report on current marketing trends?

## ❖ Delaying decision

- I think we need more time to consider this.
- I think we should postpone our decision until....
- Can we leave this until another date?
- It would be wrong to make a final decision until....

## ❖ Referring to next meeting

- We'll meet again next month to....
- We look forward to hearing from you....
- It's been a pleasure to see you today, and I look forward to our next meeting....

## ❖ Reading the minutes (notes) of the last meeting

- To begin with, I'd like to quickly go through the minutes of our last meeting.
- First, let's go over the report from the last meeting, which was held on *(date)*.
- Here are the minutes from our last meeting, which was on *(date)*.

## ❖ Closing meetings

- Let's stop here.
- I'm afraid we'll have to finish here.
- I declare the meeting closed. *(formal)*
- Let's call it a day. *(informal)*
- Well, I think that covers everything.
- I think that's about all for the time being.
- So do we agree that...?
- I'll put these proposals in writing and fax them to you tomorrow.

- ... running short on time.
- Let's wrap up our discussions.
- Just to quickly recap....
- We've basically all agreed that....
- Can you give me a show of hands....
- If no one objects, can we come back to....
- To summarize our decisions....
- Is there anything under AOB?
- Thank you for your attention.
- Thanks for coming in.

## ❖ Meeting follow-up

- ... was designated to....
- ... few details that need to be confirmed.
- Be sure to include....
- Send out the e-mail before....
- Could you repeat...?
- ... needs to be shared by....
- Make a note that....
- Does anything else need to be added?
- ... was assigned to....
- Keep the team updated on....
- Check something with....

## ❖ Meeting handouts

- Could you read over this for me?
- I would like your help proofreading this.
- This sounds right.
- Everything seems to be in order.
- Did I get everything?
- Can everyone see okay?
- Does anyone need to move to see?
- Take a handout and pass them down.
- Would you please pass down the handouts?

## ❖ Considering cultural differences

- Is there anything I should know about your country's meeting culture?
- Do you have any advice for me about your country's meeting culture?
- I'm sorry, I shouldn't have said that.
- I apologize if I was too direct.
- Why do you keep avoiding eye contact with me?
- Does eye contact make you uncomfortable?

# Appendix
# Answer Key

## Chapter.1
## Organizing meetings

### Language Practice | Page 14

1. Can you make it to the meeting on Monday?
2. We're planning on having it in the third floor conference room.
3. Could you RSVP by 5 o'clock?
4. Let me write this down.
5. Who's responsible for the agenda?
6. Could you add it to the shared agenda?
7. I'll pencil it in for next Tuesday.
8. My team is going to go over an alternative to the current marketing strategy.
9. Can you make it on Monday at 4?
10. Do you have a time preference?

#### Exercise 1
### Language Practice | Page 16

1. I am writing in response to your question about the meeting agenda.
2. I am writing to apologize for the late notice.
3. I am writing to confirm that you will be coming on Tuesday.
4. I am writing to inform you that the meeting has been changed to Conference Room B.
5. I am writing regarding the conference on Tuesday.

#### Exercise 2
### Scheduling Meetings | Page 17

**Making an appointment**
- (c) Set a date
- (e) Schedule (something in)
- (i) Set a time

**Changing an appointment**
- (a) Push back
- (h) Move forward
- (b) Postpone
- (d) Put off
- (f) Defer
- (g) Reschedule

**Exercise 3**

## Planning Agendas | Page 17

Note *Answers may vary.*

# Meeting Agenda

Date: March 9th, 2016

| | |
|---|---|
| Meeting called by | Janet Richards |
| Participants | All team leaders : Janet Richards, Bill Masters, Samuel Troy, Kevin Arnold, Emily Cooper, Jenna Smith, |
| Meeting place | 9th floor Seminar Room A |
| Start time | 14:45 |
| End time | 16:30 |
| Meeting purpose | Outline 2nd quarter project targets for each team and discuss long-term cost-cutting measures |
| Desired outcomes | Finalize 2nd quarter project targets and initiate TF for long-term cost issues |

| No. | Duration | Item | Desired Outcome | Person in charge |
|---|---|---|---|---|
| 1 | 5 minutes | Greetings and introductions | Cooperative attitude | Janet Richards |
| 2 | 15 minutes | Marketing Team A presentation | Marketing schedule plan | Kevin Arnold |
| 3 | 15 minutes | Marketing Team B presentation | Marketing project target | Jenna Smith |
| 4 | 15 minutes | Production Team A presentation | Production schedule plan | Bill Masters |
| 5 | 15 minutes | Production Team B presentation | Production project target | Samuel Troy |
| 6 | 25 minutes | Long term cost discussions | New TF | Bill Masters |
| 7 | 10 minutes | Q&A | Informed group | Janet Richards |

**Roles**

| | |
|---|---|
| Meeting preparation | Bill Masters |
| Chairperson | Janet Richards |
| Meeting minutes | Emily Cooper |
| Time keeper | Samuel Troy |

**Items to bring to the meeting**

Team project schedule ; Annual expenditure references ; Project milestones

---

**Chapter.2**

# Opening Meetings

## Language Practice | Page 24

① I'm sorry to interrupt, **could you remind me what** time this meeting is expected to finish?

② **I'd like to start by welcoming** our visitors from the Australian Branch. Mr. Jones, it's an honor to have you here.

③ Now that I have your attention, **let me begin with** the first item on the agenda.

④ As you are all aware, I've **called this meeting to** deal with some recent problems that have occurred in the customer service department.

⑤ Could I **direct your attention to the** 4th item on the agenda? I think it would be better to start with this first.

⑥ If I can get your attention, I'd like to get the meeting started.

⑦ Before we continue I'd like to clarify our roles for this meeting, Paul, **could you take the minutes?**

8. Have you all seen a copy of the agenda? If there are no questions, let's get straight into it. We want to aim for a 3pm finish.
9. Now that everyone is here and settled, let's get down to business.
10. Before we look into the first item, I'd like to briefly go over the modified budget for the second quarter.

### Exercise 1
## Greetings and Introductions | Page 26

*Note* Answers may vary.

**Formal**
- It's my honor to introduce...
- Please welcome...
- Today we have with us...
- We're very pleased to have you join us...

**Informal**
- It's good to see you...
- This is...
- ... is joining us.

**Internal Meetings**
- We have our marketing department representative...
- Please make our HR department feel welcome...

**External Meetings**
- We have ... from Corp. A, visiting us today.
- Please welcome our partners from Company B.

**First time**
- It's a pleasure to introduce... visiting for the first time from...
- We have glad to make the acquaintance...

### Exercise 3
## Greetings and Introductions | Page 27

| Chairperson | Convenes the meeting and takes responsibility in communication before and after the meeting. Leads discussions on the items of the meeting |
|---|---|
| Participant | Contributes items to meeting agenda and shares ideas in team discussions, brainstorming and the proceedings of the meeting |
| Timekeeper | Keeps track of time and reminds group of planned start and stop times for agenda items |
| Facilitator | Keeps the discussion and decision-making process moving by assisting the designated chairperson in accomplishing tasks and attending to group proceedings |
| Recorder | Keeps a written record of the meeting proceedings |
| Guest of honor | Usually an outside visitor, may or may not participate in the proceedings of the meeting |
| Secretary | Works with the chairperson to organize the meeting, is responsible for making sure that all attendees are up-to-date with the details of the meeting |

## Chapter.3
# Meeting Procedures

**Effective Meeting Skills**

### Language Practice | *Page 34*

1. Let me emphasize that we are already 2 weeks behind on this.
2. As I said earlier, it's important to get these dates fixed as soon as possible.
3. I think we're missing the point. We should be discussing the need for a new marketing strategy, not the cause and effects of micro marketing.
4. The next item on the agenda is this quarter's marketing quota.
5. Have you considered sharing the task with the production team?
6. I'm not sure what you mean by suggesting that we should change the designs.
7. I agree with the idea of outsourcing, but I think it's not a simple as it sounds.
8. Somebody mentioned something about adjusting the production schedule. Could they go into more details?
9. Can I draw your attention to the handouts?
10. I'm 100% behind you on this proposal.

**Exercise 3**

### Following Procedures | *Page 37*

**MEETING A**

<u>5</u> → <u>2</u> → <u>3</u> → <u>4</u> → <u>1</u>

**MEETING B**

<u>1</u> → <u>5</u> → <u>4</u> → <u>2</u> → <u>3</u>

**MEETING C**

<u>3</u> → <u>5</u> → <u>1</u> → <u>4</u> → <u>2</u>

**MEETING D**

<u>1</u> → <u>4</u> → <u>2</u> → <u>3</u> → <u>5</u>

## Chapter.4
# Meeting Communication

### Language Practice | *Page 44*

|  |  |  | |
|---|---|---|---|
| 1 | What about the European markets? Don't we need to readjust our marketing strategy for Europe, too? | I suggest we take that up at another meeting. It's a little off topic. | b |
| 2 | Is there anything else we need to add to this project proposal? | Could I make a suggestion? I think we should add more details about the scope of the project. | h |
| 3 | The R&D department needs to get up to date before we can arrange a meeting with the clients. | What you're saying is that the R&D department isn't prepared to be involved right away. | a |
| 4 | Do you think that our U.S. branches have enough support to work through this issue? | Good question. Let's hear what the U.S. branch managers have to say. | d |

| | | |
|---|---|---|
| 5 | We need some more ideas on how to make this product more marketable. | In my opinion, we should reevaluate our target customers for this product. — g |
| 6 | I'm sorry to interrupt, but is this procedure really necessary? We only need to review the results of the survey. | If you just let me finish, you'll know exactly what I am getting at. — c |
| 7 | We haven't heard from Sarah yet. Sarah, do you have anything to add? | No, I think you've covered everything. — e |
| 8 | What about the environmental consequences. I'm not sure this is a good idea. | I understand your concern, but I assure you that all the required environmental standards have been upheld. — f |
| 9 | Shouldn't we review last quarter's data too? I don't we have enough information to go on from here. | That's a very good point. Let's prepare a report including last quarter's data for our next meeting. — i |

**Exercise 1**

## Clarifying | Page 46

*Note Answers may vary.*

1. What you are saying is that the research is showing that UK transport planners demand motorists to pay for the use of roads directly.
2. Do you mean to say that even financial experts were unprepared for the dramatic fall in share prices?
3. That means the goods put onto the market for the first time last summer have already found plenty of buyers.
4. So what you want to say is that you are worried about the lack of improvement in the quality of work.
5. A new market investment would be a risk because of the current decline in sale figures in our existing market.
6. The productivity of the Indonesian branch and factory should not be tied with the subject of budget cuts.

# Chapter.5

# Closing Meetings

## Language Practice | Page 54

A. 3 → 2 → 1   B. 2 → 1 → 3   C. 1 → 3 → 2

D. 2 → 3 → 1   E. 1 → 3 → 2

**Exercise 1**

# Summarizing the discussion | *Page 56*

**Note** *Answers may vary.*

**Possible Meeting Summary**

### A Meeting Summary

Meeting held to review the feasibility of implementing joint-venture marketing of the online training program.

1. Marketing strategy to be developed by the R&D and Marketing Team TF. (By next Friday)
2. Research on joint-ventures, possible partner companies by the R&D Team. (Draft by next Friday)
3. Action Plan
   - Marketing strategy (As seen in item 1)
   - Technical research (As seen in item 2)
   - Update system design team for F/U marketable version of on online training program
   - Next TF meeting to be held next Friday

### B Meeting Summary

Meeting held to plan the promotion of a new product.

1. Initial trials to be held in 7 different cities.
   - San Diego, Los Angeles, Boston, Houston, Atlanta, Chicago, Philadelphia
     (Trials to start in November for 2 months)
2. Online promotions to be held for 3 weeks. In-stores promotions to be held for 2 weeks. Data comparisons to be organized by the Marketing team by Dec.
3. Promotion schedule and feedback (as above)
   - Next TF meeting to be held Nov 3$^{rd}$.

### C Meeting Summary

Meeting held to discuss increasing warehouse capacity.

1. Current warehouse capacity :
   <u>Cebu :</u> Working Capacity 10,000m$^2$
   <u>Manila :</u> Working Capacity 4,000m$^2$
   <u>Legaspi :</u> Working Capacity 24,000m$^2$
   <u>Need :</u> Addition 12,000m$^2$ for new stocks
2. Options
   - Increase Working Capacity through renovation of existing warehouse
   - Rent additional space
   - Stock take on existing warehouse products
3. Proposal to be written up and shared by next week's meeting

### D Meeting Summary

Meeting held to finalize contract terms with client.

1. Last year's price review :
   7,000 units purchased at $10.20/unit divided into 12 monthly installments for payment and delivery
2. 2016-2017 FY contract terms Upgraded model.
   9,000 units at $11.05/unit 12 monthly installments for payment and delivery Free 12 month warrantee
3. Contract details to be written up by Wednesday 19$^{th}$. Shared by fax and e-mail.

## Chapter.6

# Meeting Communication

**Language Practice** | *Page 64*

*Note* *The answers given are examples. Other answers can also be correct.*

1. James was assigned with sending out the sales reports.
2. I can check the dates with Carl, he should have the details.
3. Yes, I'll be sure to keep the team updated on the project.
4. There are a few details that need to be confirmed before I send out the e-mail.
5. Be sure to include a timeline for completing the action plans in the e-mail.
6. I was designated to write up the meeting minutes and share them over our intranet.
7. We told them that we would send out an e-mail before lunch tomorrow.
8. Sorry, could you repeat that last part again?
9. The report needs to be shared by 3 in the afternoon.

Exercise 2

## Meeting Minutes Do's & Don'ts | *Page 67*

**Do**

- Be concise. All you are required to do is to convey the essence of the meeting to its attendees and non-attendees in a brief format.
- Spell out acronyms and abbreviations, at least when you use them for the first time in the text.
- Be specific. Otherwise, it will be difficult for the readers of your meeting minutes to understand the circumstances that led to the decision.
- Use bulleted lists when specifying comments, suggestions or decisions made.

**Don't**

- Describe emotions of the attendees. Meeting minutes are supposed to be a concise and accurate document that refers only to business.
- Include any personal opinions about the happenings in the meeting.
- Report on every little detail in your meeting minutes.

## Chapter 7

# Roles and Responsibilities

**Exercise 2**

### How to... (Skill 2)

- **H** Planning every detail ahead of time.
- **B** Showing up at the agreed upon time.
- **B** Bringing any necessary materials.
- **B** Listening to presenters' contributions.
- **H** Maintaining the flow of the meeting.
- **H** Introducing attendees to one another.
- **H** Writing and sharing the meeting minutes.
- **B** Taking notes when necessary.
- **H** Deciding on the structure of the meeting.
- **G** Asking questions to further your understanding.

## Chapter 8

# Setting and Environment

**Exercise 1**

### How to... (Skill 1)

*Note* Answers may vary.

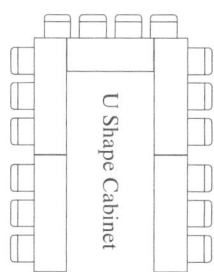

A U-shape Cabinet is recommended.

**Exercise 2**

### How to... (Skill 2)

*Note* Answers may vary.

- **O** Vacation plans
- **O** A mutual acquaintance
- **O** Recent weather
- **O** A sports championship
- **X** A mistake a presenter made
- **X** Local election results
- **X** Company layoffs
- **O** An upcoming long weekend
- **O** An interesting picture on the wall
- **O** Children's accomplishments

# Chapter.9
# Writing Technique

**Exercise 2**

**How to...** *(Skill 2)*

Note *Answers may vary.*

1. Janet Adams called a vote on assigning a research team to determine the cost of breaking ground on the Linden Avenue project. The motion passed 9 to 1.
2. Ben Richards called a vote on postponing until next week. The vote passed.
3. Alex Reed was assigned to take over the Clayton account. The meeting was adjourned.
4. The chair went over the agenda.

# Chapter.10
# Meeting Etiquette

**Exercise 2**

**How to...** *(Skill 2)*

1. C  2. E  3. A  4. G  5. B
6. D  7. F

# Chapter.11
# Cross-Cultural Skills

**Exercise 1**

**How to...** *(Skill 1)*

1. C  2. E  3. G  4. D  5. F
6. B  7. H  8. A